Faith and Freedom

Exploring Radical Orthodoxy

EDITED BY

Jeremy Morris

Affirming Catholicism

third millennium

AFFIRMING CATHOLICISM
(Registered Charity no. 1007291)
St Matthew's House · 20 Great Peter Street · London SW1P 2BU
Tel: +44 (0) 20 7222 5166

Journal Editor: Jeremy Morris

Reviews Editor: James Garrard

Third Millennium is the Journal of Affirming Catholicism in a new format. It is published three times a year as a continuing series of books – each on a selected theme. Volumes will contain substantial essays on the theme, as well as book reviews, information, letters and other material.

All views expressed in *Third Millennium* are those of the named authors alone and cannot be taken to reflect the policy of Affirming Catholicism. We retain the right to edit contributions and to exercise discretion over all material submitted for publication.

Articles for *Third Millennium* are always welcome. Submissions should be clearly titled and should bear the name of the author. Sources of all quotations and references must be noted in full. Please send a hard copy of the article and, if possible, a disk containing a file of the text in digital format, together with a covering letter giving an address and daytime telephone number.

The address to which articles, reviews and any other correspondence should be sent is: The Revd Dr Jeremy Morris, Trinity Hall, Cambridge CB2 1TJ.

DESIGN: Helen Robertson
COPY-EDITING AND TYPESETTING: Special Edition Pre-press Services
PRINTED IN ENGLAND BY MPG Books

ISSN 1468-9413

Third Millennium 6, September 2003
© 2003 Affirming Catholicism

Contents

Editor's Introduction   1
JEREMY MORRIS

Is Orthodoxy Radical?   5
CATHERINE PICKSTOCK

Barth, Hegel and the possibility for
     Christian apologetics   17
GRAHAM WARD

Reading the Bible Theologically:
     Text, Church and Life   39
EDMUND NEWEY

Radical Orthodoxy: A Review   49
SIMON OLIVER

Theological Integrity: A Brief Introduction
     to the Thought of Rowan Williams   61
EDMUND NEWEY

A Sermon in Season – SIMON OLIVER   71

Book Reviews (listed overleaf)   75

Book Reviews

Stanley Hauerwas · *With the Grain of the Universe*   75

Tom Wright · *The Resurrection of the Son of God*   77

Susan Frank Parsons (ed) · *The Cambridge
Companion to Feminist Theology*   81

Adrian Hastings · *Oliver Tomkins.
The Ecumenical Enterprise*   84

F. D. Maurice · *The Kingdom of Christ;
The Prayer Book; Theological Essays*   86

Steven Croft · *Transforming Communities.
Re-imagining the Church for the 21st Century*   87

Editor's Introduction

What is it that sets religious people off from others? Or, should I say, explicitly religious people? Is it greater purity of life? Is it a wholly different set of interests? Is it contempt for others? Is it belonging to a subculture? It is all or some or none of these things, depending on who you are, your prejudices and predilections, your background, and so on. In fact, merely to pose the question is to risk criticism – unless, that is, it leads to the obvious answer, the pious and yet authentic answer that it is the beliefs professed that set religious people apart. Christians are no different from others, then, except that they profess belief in Jesus Christ as incarnate Son of God, who died to save us from our sins. Well, no different – that is, no better intrinsically, not superior, not 'special' in the eyes of others. But, yes different, because the beliefs demand practice and should then encompass a distinctive scale of values and a quality of living, or approach to living.

Practically, this ambiguity about Christian difference makes life uncomfortable for Christians, who – if sincere and, within the limits of their own nature, devout – are always striving both to be the kind of people we think Christ wants us to be and at the same time to resist the spiritual pride that can so easily follow. But what is difficult for us as individuals is correspondingly difficult for the Church as a whole in society. Once, public sensibility was at least realistic about the possibility of Christians' failure. Clerical misdemeanours were always scandalous. There were always hypocrites. There was always abuse. There was always vindictiveness, greed and misdirected zeal. But the general assumption was that, despite this, the Church was sufficiently necessary to the well-being of society, sufficiently close to the truth of life in general, that the benefits it brought society as a whole evidently outweighed the consequences of its failures. In fact, what now looks like an unacceptable 'hiding' of failure might also have been an attempt – however misguided – to contain and manage failure, in order that the values the Church promoted for the flourishing of society as a whole might not suffer irreversible damage. I said 'might also have been an attempt' because it is always unsatisfactory to reduce complex motivation to a one-dimensional account – to say that it was 'simply this' or 'simply that', simply a cover-up or simply the best way of dealing with things.

What one can't help but be aware of today is that there is no longer any consensus about the benefits of religion to society at large. There are plenty of people hostile to religion altogether. For them, religion may be positively harmful. Scandal and hypocrisy don't happen in spite of good intentions – they demonstrate the false, illusory nature of Christian values. For many others, the good intentions stand, and religion has its place in promoting them, but not at the expense of other people's freedoms. Religion, for them, is all right 'so far as it goes'. But it doesn't go very far beyond a 'private' realm, where its value is located. It doesn't have much of a public role. For others still – probably for many reading these words – religion is still a question of public truth and public value, at least to the extent that churches promote values of sociability, 'love in action', forgiveness and peace that ought to be central to the way our society is structured. Churches can, then, cooperate with other religions, and good people of other views, on certain common tasks. Probably fewer of us still would make the stronger claim still that Christianity represents ultimate and essential social truth – though that is a logical and persuasive implication of what we believe.

The difficulty of the Church's situation today is that, of the four views I've outlined above, neither the third nor the fourth represents anything like a dominant view in public life. On the contrary, the second – the 'religion within its limits', or 'private religion' – probably holds most sway, at least for the negative reason that, whatever people think about Christianity *per se*, a much more pervasive ethical principle today is that everyone is entitled to their own opinion, and no one opinion should be promoted above others. For – so the argument runs – promotion of one person's opinion represents the demotion (and so restriction) of another's. This dubious piece of logic is the unfortunate consequence of the battle for freedom of opinion that first occurred amongst Christians themselves in the nineteenth century, as they argued over the scope and rights of Establishment. They shared a great deal in common, and so it was possible to conduct arguments for and against the public endorsement of religious faith without doing serious damage to the assumption that, despite disagreement, Britain was a recognizably Christian state. But, as that breadth of agreement on common Christianity receded in the late twentieth century, what was left were the negative implications that attached to defence of freedom of opinion. Arguably, that opened the door for the first view, too.

And yet this reluctance to recognize the public claims of religion has become embedded in the common view of our culture and, by extension, our history. The result is a terrible aphasia, a forgetting of the religious experience that has infused our national history for most of its course. It has longed since ceased to be fashionable or persuasive to see English literature as a literature provoked or inspired, for the most part, by religious arguments. Yet, until the twentieth century, most of our great poets, novelists and musicians wrote out of Christian conviction. Not just Donne, Herbert and Cowper – the usual suspects – but virtually all the others in some sense were writing within the Christian tradition. Perhaps Byron, Shelley, Clough and Swinburne were the notable exceptions (and even then that is only half true), but basically the history of English literature is a history of Christian sensibility, in all its diversity, conflict and change. Yet this rarely registers today.

For all sorts of reasons – not least the pluralism of British society – it is undesirable and impossible simply to return to the basic Christian consensus that once underpinned our national culture. But there is, all the same, something to be said for a renewed conviction that Christian faith has public resonance, and a renewed determination not to concede ground to arguments that have little or nothing to contribute to the Christian vision of human wellbeing. As a matter of historical justice, the weight of the Christian tradition in our national culture needs to be recognized once more. Paradoxically, that requires new emphases, and new methods of theological exposition, precisely in order to accent the continuing relevance of Christian orthodoxy. That is where the 'movement' called Radical Orthodoxy, highlighted in this issue, for all its controversial character has much to excite us. It bids us be much more sceptical of the dominant ways of thinking in our national culture today. It is, for all that, sharp, provocative and challenging. It will invite disagreement, doubtless. But it may also provoke curiosity, and even assent.

Jeremy Morris

Is Orthodoxy Radical?

CATHERINE PICKSTOCK

Orthodoxy is not a book of rules or a series of defined proposi-
tions. It is the organic language of tradition, a language
whose use has been increasingly curtailed as modern
life with its typical confidence and hubristic rationalism
has taken over almost all of our thought processes and
assumptions – and in spite of the limitations and possibly
even the failure of the whole modernist project to which the
arrival of 'postmodernism' (with its focus on details and
signs and its rejection of context) seems to bear witness.

Since the 1960s, the mood of theology has undergone an important change. Up until then, theologians tended to take modernity,
and even the secularization of many spheres of life, for granted.
These new spheres were frequently regarded as an outcome
of Christianity itself, and often of Protestantism in particular.
The modern secular world was seen in terms of humanity's
having come of age, of God having handed over to humanity the
responsibility for the worldly order. This was coordinated with a
suggestion that the real God was a retired God, distant and secret,
and, at the same time, paradoxically, a God identical with the very
world from which he had retired. These developments reached an
extreme pitch with the so-called 'death of God' theology which
sought to suggest that God was most disclosed when he was no
longer held to exist as an objective metaphysical reality. Once
this point had been reached, theology had nowhere further to go,
unless it radically changed direction and started to question the
hegemony of the secular and the modern. Such questioning was
encouraged by developments within the secular world itself; the
post-war consensus world of social democracy and the welfare
state started to come unstuck. A far bleaker world of market

competition and naked individualism had begun to take its place. These unsettling processes commenced during the 1970s and reached a crescendo during the Thatcherite era. Suddenly, it no longer seemed as if there were a shared ground between right-thinking agnostics and humanists on the one hand and religious people on the other. With astonishing rapidity, even self-described Marxists started to explain that an increasing role for the market economy and unleashing of individualism was a 'necessary stage' in human development. Many of them later affirmed that it was not even a stage but the final goal itself. Throughout the 1980s it was no accident that the most vigorous opposition to Thatcherism came from the bishops of the Church of England. They cleaved still to the vision enshrined in the post-war settlement.

However, these bishops longed, on the whole, for the old consensus between all right-thinking people. For younger theologians, however much they might admire the stance taken by people such as the late Lord Runcie, things appeared rather differently. They started to realize that the old consensus, which enshrined collective values and a concern for the common good, was much more of an echo of a religious world view than had been fully admitted. Now, by contrast, secularism was emerging in its full, vivid colours. This meant a celebration of individualism and brutal competition, only qualified by a perceived need to instil discipline into poorer people who might otherwise protest against their lot – one is thinking here of the often hypocritical combination of liberal economic values with conservative social policy. Younger theologians, therefore, were starting to face in two apparently contradictory directions. On the one hand, they remained committed to the broadly Christian socialist vision of many Anglican leaders of the twentieth century, in traditions stretching back to Gore, Westcott and the more radical Stewart Headlam. On the other hand, the alliance of collective politics with modernity and progress no longer seemed so obvious; to the contrary, they started to wonder whether such collectivism was not necessarily upheld by a sense of a religious destiny reaching beyond the mere selfish and ephemeral imagined desires of individuals. For this reason, as well as for many others, they were increasingly drawn back to a pre-modern theology.

Such developments, ever since the 1970s, were particularly in evidence in Cambridge, nurtured especially by the new Archbishop of Canterbury, Rowan Williams. They were further enshrined in his pupil John Milbank's book, *Theology and Social Theory* (1990).[1] Radical orthodoxy emerged some years after Milbank had returned to teach at Cambridge. A feeling arose amongst several people, myself included – some of us still at that time students, others lecturers and quite a number from elsewhere in Britain and the USA – that we had all begun to pursue theology in a slightly different way, and that the already established combination of traditional theology and collectivist politics had begun to assume a new and distinctive form. A meeting was held to see if this was indeed the case, and from it, certain themes emerged which later formed the basis of a collection of essays entitled *Radical Orthodoxy* (1999).[2]

Amongst these themes one was fundamental. To the mix of orthodoxy and political radicalism had been added, by a new generation, a third ingredient, namely, postmodernism. It is perhaps notable that despite an initial association of the postmodern with the free market, the current attempt by Tony Blair to take forward the liberalization of every aspect of society is promoted in the name of modernity. For it seems that this ignores the way in which there has been a loss of confidence in the project of modernity ever since the 1960s. This has been manifest in many different ways. People no longer think that once constraints on reason have been removed reason will disclose to us the way things really are. Scientists are no longer confident that there are fixed objective laws in nature or that they can gradually progress towards a full disclosure of the workings of nature. Philosophers are increasingly aware that all thought proceeds within certain subjective assumptions. Ethicists realize that there cannot be a common human basis for moral values outside the diversity of different traditions and different visions of human life which go beyond the adjudications of reason. Even secular people, if they are reflective, feel ambivalent about the loosening grip of religion, narrative, tradition and community. No longer do they suppose that emancipation from these things will produce liberal, rational, reasonable people. Instead, it seems to produce frightened, deracinated people, who are easily prey to media manipulation, and the scape-goating of classes and figures who are blamed for all our ills. Emancipated people, it transpires, are often those with no memory and no resources for deep reflection. In the face of what has been described as the culture of narcissism, many thinkers have proclaimed the value of the local, the specific, the particular, of 'thick' traditions gathered around shared mythic narratives and inherited rituals which exceed reason and yet seem to produce an order more reasonable than reason alone could bring about. Often this mood has led to the celebration of difference which characterizes postmodern philosophy. The search for some underlying real universal truth is now held to be 'bad' and oppressive. All there is is the diversity of signs and symbols on the surface. This is our real, variegated humanity, and emancipation now means releasing that, rather than paving the way for the vision of a single enlightened truth.

In the last few years, some theologians at Cambridge and elsewhere have inevitably been influenced by this new mood. The hero was no longer Marx but Nietzsche. And, suddenly, the big task of a previous generation of theologians seemed to make no immediate sense. That task had been to 'reconcile Christianity with the Enlightenment; to make it compatible with modernity'. But now, even secular people begin to doubt modernity; it would be apparent just how deeply confusing this is – and remains – for an earlier generation of theologians, and even many of their younger followers. The reason for the passionate opposition to so-called 'post-secular theology', including radical orthodoxy, is that liberal theologians find it hard to accept that the very name of the game has changed. They knew where they were with straightforward old-time conservatives. What they do not necessarily receive so warmly is the confusing combination of pre-modern theology, postmodern philosophy and left-wing politics.

The combination of these three elements is partly what makes radical orthodoxy distinct from other recent movements in theology (such as the Yale School, Radical Traditions at Duke University, and Scriptural Reasoning associated with Peter

Ochs at the University of Virginia). But surely there is a further ingredient to add? For postmodern theologians are two-a-penny. If radical orthodoxy were postmodern, it would be nothing new; and there would be nowhere further for it to go. Postmodern theologians, indeed, cannot bear the sight of us. Why is this? The reason is complicated, but, put briefly, radical orthodoxy argues that postmodernity only witnesses to the negative failure of modernity. The postmodern stance towards the local traditions it recommends is an avowedly ironic one. And, in fact, it assumes that because universal reason is an illusion, differences are bound to be in conflict, while the illusory search for the universal can never be halted. Difference can never fully arrive. The world is bound to be conflictual. The order through chaos of the market is the best that we can do, even if postmodernists hope somehow for a less monopolistic market than we have at present. Most postmodern theologians just go along with this. They simply add that difference is God and God is difference.

Now, radical orthodoxy believes that God is difference as well. But we also believe that God created the world in such a way that its differences exist in harmony, even if this order has been interrupted by the disorder of the Fall. Radical orthodoxy further believes that monotheistic faith has always imagined differences in harmony. This harmony remains mysterious and never fully graspable because it derives from the transcendent God. Thus, one is not faced with the alternative, either graspable universal reason or else anarchic chaos of variety. We instead insist upon an understanding of local differences in their integrity as partial strivings towards something greater. Thus, the genius of catholic Christianity has been to allow local traditions to fulfil themselves in adding their own particular glosses upon Christian ceremony and tradition.

In this way, radical orthodoxy is both with and against post-modernism: against, because we think that differences, to be real differences, must co-exist, otherwise they would simply contest each other and vanish under the freight of agonism; but we are with postmodernism because we find there an affinity with the pre-modern in supposing that we live in a surface world of shifting and mysterious signs and symbols that we must constantly seek to decipher. This is the world created *ex nihilo*, for, as Augustine said, things in themselves are nothing; they only consist in a shadowy reflection of God, their Creator. Postmodernism, by contrast, takes a more nihilistic stance: there is nothing beneath the drift of signs. Radical orthodoxy seeks to reposition this nihilism: the flux of signs is only not nothing because it reflects God who is everything. Thus, there is no secure secular escape from anarchy, the indeterminacy of meaning. But there is a theological escape: everything participates in God; meaning is open-ended but not drifting in a void; we trust that we are being led above ourselves to a vision we cannot yet attain. The 'nothing' from which we are all created is not the void of postmodernism but the inexhaustible plenitude of God, dark only by excess of light.

The watchword of radical orthodoxy, beyond postmodernism, is participation, a Platonic framework which was developed by Christianity as well as by Judaism and Islam. According to this framework, because everything derives from God, it derives traces of the divine reality. Everything shows us a little of what God is like. Although this means that matter points above itself to a spiritual realm, the view elevates and does not denigrate matter. The spiritual tree is even more tree than the material tree; that is to say, the tree in the mind of God loses nothing of bark and leaf, not to mention swings and tree houses. However, radical orthodoxy holds that the loss of the doctrine of participation in the later middle ages is responsible for much of our contemporary confusion. Beginning most markedly with Duns Scotus, though with many earlier anticipations, and carried further by William of Ockham, two theoretical shifts began to occur: first, people started to think that one could talk adequately about the content of things without reference to God. For example, one could describe a tree, or describe what it is to be true or good simply in finite terms. One would afterwards append the idea that God had created the tree, and so on, as if He were just another individual, only rather bigger and cleverer. Secondly, and closely linked, because the tree can be described without reference to God, according to such a view, it necessarily shows us nothing about God; God has made trees, goodness, and so on, but this does not mean that God is in any way eminently tree-y or good, in our human sense, at all. As a result of these developments, further consequences follow. Human beings, in the image of God, began to be thought of as autonomous wills, and human society began to be seen as a collection of isolated atoms. So one can see that the loss of participation, in the metaphysical sense, leads to the loss of participation in a more familiar political sense. The secularization of the Western world leads directly to political individualism and a doctrine of selfishness. Furthermore, when God and the tree are only linked by efficient causality, a new dualism starts to emerge. The spiritual and the material become two separate realms; bodies start to have nothing to do with the soul; religion becomes an internal, private affair. But radical orthodoxy has sought to show that this does not lead to a preservation of the integrity of bodily life. Instead, it leads to its denigration. For, according to this duality, bodily things are those which will pass away. The only things now trusted to be permanent are abstract laws and signs by which bodies are regulated. A spatial grid of formal positions remains. Think perhaps of the way in which, though people die one by one, the abstract population level remains abiding. By contrast, if bodies are seen to participate in God, they have eternal significance, and are seen in the light of their resurrection. For a more nihilistic outlook, bodies fade into nothing and are therefore defined by that nothingness. But for a Christian outlook, bodies persist in the plenitude of the creator. Perhaps one could go as far as to say that Christianity – and not atheism – is the real materialism!

Does all this, however, mean that radical orthodoxy views modernity in entirely negative terms – as the time of the loss of participation? Is it an essentially nostalgic movement? The answer is no, because there is another aspect to modernity which we celebrate. Starting from well before 1300, and continuing through the Renaissance and the Enlightenment, human beings started to become more and more aware of their potential creatively to transform themselves and the world for human benefit and the greater beautification of life. Humanity as maker emerged, and the capacities of both art and science were vastly expanded. However, this development was interpreted in two different ways. On the whole, and unfortunately, it occurred in a way which denied participation. On this understanding, human creativity does not participate in God's creativity – to the contrary, it carves out an autonomous domain for itself within finite being taken as fully Being. Within this domain, human will, power and knowledge are absolute – the equal of God's, though within a finite compass. Thus, Galileo declared that we know the laws of logic, mathematics and even physics just as well as God does. Such a view opened up the possibility of a purely instrumental approach to nature and society, ignoring the way that both may disclose the divine. On the other hand, a minority tradition (exemplified by Nicholas of Cusa, and many Augustinian humanists) interpreted human productive power as a participation in the Father's creative utterance of the Logos. For this view, human productive understanding remains conjectural and approximative. Moreover, human artistry does not here open out a sphere of command but instead gropes to realize the full human telos and to make more manifest divine revelation.

For radical orthodoxy, the challenge is to take up again this minority tradition which represents a kind of counter-modernity. This means we wish to proclaim the liberation of human powers, but at the same time, to regard their development as an increased attention to divine purposes which lie forever beyond us.

However, the predominant modern tradition abandoned parti-cipation. This now engendered a further duality, namely, one between faith and reason. If the tree no longer shows a trace of the divine, then one had to reason back to God as efficient cause of the tree by a cold objective reason uninformed by the divine light of illumination, which surely is already faith? And from this it was but a short step to the conclusion that objective reason did not point to God as efficient cause at all. To supplement the poverty of the knowledge of God, delivered by reason, or the complete lack of any knowledge at all, faith had to be evoked. But this too was no longer mediated by a restoration of the image of God in human will, power and reason. Instead, it was now a kind of arbitrary act of willed assent to certain divinely revealed facts or propositions instilled by clerical or else Biblical authority.

How did this differ from the earlier order of things? Reason had previously been seen as requiring a kind of faith or advance knowledge of what one is reasoning about; this is the case for

Augustine, Anselm and Aquinas. Conversely, faith had been seen as but the restoration of our natural reason which, as natural, is yet orientated to the supernatural beatific vision. A radically orthodox perspective is perhaps primarily characterized by a new refusal of the modern duality of faith and reason. This is why it has been termed 'a new theology' and why the orthodoxy is 'radical'. Hitherto, theologians have tended to be either liberals, who stress reason, or conservatives and neo-orthodox, who stress faith. By contrast, the French theologian Henri de Lubac already started to contest this duality, and radical orthodoxy has sought to carry his arguments further. However, in this respect, it is characteristically Anglican. There is a myth which says 'Catholics stress Church hierarchy; Protestants stress the Bible; Anglicans stress Reason'. This is not, however, necessarily the case. Anglicans have always stressed the indivisibility of faith and reason, from Hooker, through Cudworth to Coleridge, F. D. Maurice and John Henry Newman. But in doing so they have sustained a certain fidelity to Patristic and high mediaeval theology up to the time of Aquinas. One hastens to add, however, that many, many individuals in the Roman Catholic and Protestant Churches have also exhibited this fidelity.

This leads me to another crucial characteristic of radical orthodoxy. Most theologies begin by being rooted in one specific church tradition. Radical orthodoxy, however, was born as an ecumenical theology. Its first contributors happened to be Anglicans and Roman Catholics. But it now has Eastern Orthodox, Methodist, Presbyterian and Baptist sympathizers. The latter may seem surprising, as it makes no bones about being a Catholic movement, yet it is notable that today many Protestant churches are seeking to retrieve a broader catholicity. Although radical orthodoxy has been criticized for being too narrow and even anti-Protestant, this is to ignore the point that it has a specific ecumenical proposal to make. It invites both Protestants and post-Tridentine Roman Catholics to examine the extent to which they remain embroiled in early modern disputes; and, indeed, to realize that their differences themselves result from late mediaeval Scholastic confusions. We do not, however, claim any originality for this proposal. It has been brewing in much twentieth century historical theology, both Protestant and Roman Catholic. We simply wish to make it more explicit.

Nevertheless, you may be asking yourselves, this is all very well, but why 'orthodoxy'? Doesn't that mean a set of rigid doctrines and propositions? To which one must answer that Christian doctrine is itself grounded in the kind of vision of creation and participation and illumination so far given. Christian doctrine developed in the first few centuries not as a set of positive items on a checklist, but as a series of negative safeguards for a staggeringly radical vision.

For this vision, God in Himself is relational; God in Himself cannot be without His own image and without a desire even in excess of that image. God is the mystery of signs; God is the mystery of a gift exchanged, and non-identically repeated. That is the mystery of the Trinity. God is not a being but Being as such. But Being as such is word and gift as well as origin; it is community and not isolated individuality. This infinite plenitude gives the world. The world begins as an excess without laws. It begins with freely offered gifts and demands from human beings only celebration and worship, which constitute the reception of those gifts. Inexplicably, however, God's gift to us was refused, and we live within a shattered offering. And yet it is impossible for God to be thwarted. He goes on giving. Since the world is now distanced from Him by its refusal of Him, he must enter into the world to show us the truth. Body separated from God perishes. So God becomes embodied; he becomes incarnate. After the Fall, our reason is confused, and must be re-educated by our bodies and our senses. God comes to dwell in a body and lives as a vagrant travelling, celebrating, healing, accompanied by prostitutes, criminals and foreigners. Our senses must respond to this if we are to be saved. But God was captured and crucified by human reason erecting its laws on its own account, in continued refusal of the divine gift. God's manifestation of Himself in a joyful, peaceful community, healing nature, restoring harmony with nature, feeding the hungry, healing the sick, above all, exchanging gifts, was refused. However, in this final refusal even of God Himself, God is still given. The broken God is the resurrected God whom we still receive in the Eucharist. This is the God entirely offered to us. To this God, we entirely offer ourselves and receive ourselves again. This is the economy of always excessive giving and forgiving without exception and beyond the law. This is the excessive divine economy; it is God's offering to us of a just community based upon collective sharing and the search for common purpose.

The foregoing is a short description of why orthodoxy is perforce radical; and an attempt to give some sense of how radical orthodoxy cleaves to the Christian socialist vision in terms which do not rest within a postmodern outlook.

But, you may be asking, what difference can this make for me? And here, finally, one must touch upon the implications of radical orthodoxy for the life of the institutional church. I have referred to participation in God as necessarily involving social participation. Christianity points to a renewed community. But this is not the Church's teaching to society; instead, the Church itself is the initial site of this renewed community. Church is the name for the beginnings of the eschatological kingdom. And it is this site especially because participation in God is not mainly an abstruse metaphysical doctrine; it is something only fulfilled and realized as worship. A tree worships God by being true to its tree-ness, rain by being rain-y. And human beings by being human; but that means by being liturgical creatures, going beyond ourselves to give ourselves back to God. We can try as hard as we like to reach God in private meditation, but in the end, we must go beyond this to reach out towards the ungraspable in words and songs and gestures of praise, in the hope that God will meet us in these gestures. Worship, then, is not so much the beginning but the end, or rather, the anticipation of the end. In the same way, worship does not improve the quality of our collective life. It is the end of collective life. The basis of a just society is to be found when we take the surplus of our work and production and collectively shape it into something beautiful and visible by the divine. Perhaps one can think here of the astonishing figures of birds, miles long and miles wide, in the Peruvian desert, created by prehistoric man and only visible as birds in the twentieth century from the air (though of course the angels have seen them for many centuries). We need to recover a sense of true ritual in liturgy, a sense of something which is beautiful, constantly repeated, yet always repeated with difference. We need to recover a sense that all our work and life together feeds into liturgical offering towards God. Above all, we need to recover a sense that charity, as Rowan Williams has said, is finally play, the exchange of gifts, and a sense that, since human labour produces more than is necessary, this excess is not for a dull stockpiling of wealth but rather for a joyful offering to God which sustains the play of divine–human interchange. In this way, we can recover the radicalism of orthodoxy. We need, all of us, in small ways, to interrupt the deadly seriousness of secular life which cannot even take leisure lightly and increasingly demands that everyone work all the time. This deadly seriousness is, ironically, the outcome of selfish greed which ignores collective well-being. Without social participation we become overworked, bored and miserable. But the only ground for social participation is participation in the triune life of God.

Catherine Pickstock is a lecturer in the philosophy of religion at Cambridge University and a Fellow of Emmanuel College.

NOTES

1   John Milbank, *Theology and Social Theory: Beyond Secular Reason* (Oxford: Blackwell, 1990).

2   John Milbank, Catherine Pickstock and Graham Ward (eds), *Radical Orthodoxy: A New Theology* (London: Routledge, 1999).

Barth, Hegel and the possibility for Christian apologetics

GRAHAM WARD

Why does the possibility of Christian apologetics matter? Any attempt to answer this question requires considering the nature and significance of theological discourse, and that consideration in turn requires thinking through the context in which such discourse arises. For whom is theology written and for what purpose? Or, who does the theologian address and what is the task undertaken in the address? Christian apologetics situates the theological task with respect to the gospel of salvation in Christ freely offered to the world – a world not divorced from Christ but whose meaning is only known with respect to Christ as the one through whom all things were made and have their being. As such, apologetics orientates theological discourse towards a specific cultural and historical negotiation concerning public truth. Its task is evangelical and doxological. Upon the basis of apologetics rests, then, the Christian mission not only to disseminate the good news but to bring about cultural and historical transformations concomitant with the coming of the Kingdom of God. This is why the possibility for Christian apologetics matters – for its task makes manifest the polity of the Christian gospel, its moral, social and political orders. Its task is Christological insofar as it is the continuation of, and participation in, the redemptive work of Christ. Without the orientation of Christian apologetics towards the world, the theological task is merely an exercise in navel-gazing. And while a reflexivity has necessarily to be intrinsic to theological work – for the theologian attempts to speak in the name of Christ, and that is a presumption the theologian must continually be scandalized by – that reflexivity cannot be the *telos* of the theological work.

The possibility for a Christian apologetics then is fundamental to the theological task. Apologetics have a theological war-rant for the work they undertake in the operation of the Word in the salvation of the world. But they have no unmediated access to that Word such that it can be wielded like a weapon or used like a tool. The basis upon which apologetics engage the Word with the world requires an understanding of both the character of that Word and the character of the world. This dual understanding involves an immersion in the words and works that bear witness to the Word and the words and works that characterize any particular cultural context. And here lies the risk, the dialectical risk that theology must run. On the one hand, in understanding the world theology comes to understand itself (what it has to say, what is the *charism* it has been given to deliver). In understanding itself, it must receive the revelation of Christ that comes from that time and place 'before the foundations of the world'. It must participate in that grace whereby the eternal makes provision for and maintains the temporal, challenging all that is fallen and misconceived. On the other hand, the theologian is situated within the world. Being situated in the world at a particular time, in a particular cultural situation, he or she takes up the theological task with the resources of the tradition and a mind-set formed in and through the words and works that constitute this *habitus*. The theologian can only understand the faith held and practised by the Christian church, the theological task this enjoins and the people to whom this task is addressed, through what is culturally and historically available. The theo-logic of theology itself, the faith that seeks understanding, is then constituted in a cultural negotiation between the revelation of Christ to the Church (rooted in the Scriptures, the sacraments and the tra-dition of their interpretation and application) and the 'signs of the times'. Both the danger and the possibility of apologetics lie in the degree of critical difference between the Christian *evan-gelium* and the ways in which the world produces and main-tains its own historical self-reflection. But, and this remains fundamental, neither can be accessed without the other. The secular world is never confronted as such without first being constructed as a homogenous cultural order from the standpoint of Christian difference; while the Christian difference is never defined as such without also being constructed as a homogeneous religious culture from the standpoint of the irreligious or de-divinized world-view. This is why, in attempting to demonstrate the necessity of Christian apologetics, and its possibility, the work of Karl Barth is important. For Barth, while opposing dogmatics as the study of God's self-revelation in the service of the Church to the *Kulturprotestantismus* of apologetics, not only alerts the Christian theologian to the dangers of such a project but, in his dialectical method, performs his own wrestling with the relation between the Word of God and the words and works of the world.[1]

'[A]s long as he [*sic*] is an apologist the theologian must renounce his theological function,' Barth writes in one of his perceptive analyses of Schleiermacher (Barth, 2001, 428).[2] He thought Schleiermacher had failed as a theologian on exactly this score, and led many another nineteenth-century theologian in tow. As his own two-fold introduction to the *Church Dogmatics* – 'The Task of Dogmatics' and 'The Task of Prolegomena to Dogmatics' – makes plain, theology may be exegetical, dogmatic or practical, but since its task is to examine 'the agreement of the Church's distinctive talk about God with the being of the Church' it has no role to play *vis-à-vis* the 'secular or pagan' (*CD*, I.1, 4–5). Theology so conceived speaks from faith to faith. Where it involves itself with unbelief, it is not 'pure unbelief' (*CD*, I.1, 32), but those forms of unbelief within the Church itself, within interpretations of the faith, among heresies. But the seriousness with which unbelief has to be taken when it lies outside the Church or interpretations of the faith, means that, first, it cannot take the theological task itself 'with full seriousness' (*CD*, I.1, 30) and, second, can only proceed on the assumption that the dogmatic task of the faith coming to an understanding of itself is completed. The theologian, therefore, compromises himself or herself when 'He [*sic*] must present himself to [the educated among the despisers of religion] in a part which is provided for in their categories' (Barth, 2001, 428). Where the task of theology accomplishes a genuine apologetics, it does so only as a by-product of its exegetical, dogmatic and practical tasks. This genuine apologetics is recognized by its effectiveness. That is, it produces an event of faith that is otherwise beyond all human polemical endeavours; the work of theology is 'empowered and blessed by God as the witness of faith' (*CD*, I.1, 31). This effect cannot be prescribed or planned for in advance. The unbeliever overhears a conversation internal to faith seeking its own understanding through which occurs the speaking of God's Word, a revelation that 'itself creates of itself the necessary point of contact' (*CD*, I.1, 29).

If theological apologetics is to avoid the construction of follies, it must examine why it can speak, and speak not only to, for and in the Church, but to, for and in the world beyond the Church. Theology needs to expound the grounds for why it can be apologetic without ceasing, in that task, to be theological. And again Barth is important here, because he himself asked these questions – even if we may decide to depart from both the answers he gave to, and his framing of, those questions. Weaving in and out of a conversation with Barth, what kind of a theological basis for apologetics can be found?

Much of Barth's polemic against apologetics and *Kultur- protestantismus* is a mellower form of the 'infinite qualitative difference' between God's Word and human words found in his commentaries upon Romans. There, in his first commentary (1919) he could announce, 'That you as Christians are to have nothing to do [*nichts zu tun habt*] with monarchism, capitalism, militarism, patriotism and liberalism is so obvious that I need not say anything' (Barth, 1963, 381). Proclaiming the new world in Christ, and God's counter-cultural NO – intensified in the second edition of the commentary – Barth's eschatological fervour was reactive, and addressed explicitly to the Protestant theologians he felt had betrayed the *evangelium*. But it is exactly at the point of what Christians are to do or not do that a theological analysis aware of its own cultural embeddedness has to begin. For Barth's sentiment in the first editions of *Romans* is naïve, but the grounds upon which it is naïve need to be made explicit. It is the very fact that Christians act [*zu tun*] in the world, even if their actions are graced and therefore eschatologically informed, that means they cannot be inoculated against an involvement in 'monarchism, capitalism, militarism, patriotism and liberalism.' Barth's radical separatism, at this point in his work, betrays, in fact, an inadequate mode of dialectical thinking.[3] It is inadequate because it is unable to think through the relationship of this God of cultural judgement to Barth's equal insistence, against Harnack among others, that Christians are not neutral subjects in the events of the world; they cannot remain indifferent to the social, political and economic circumstances in which they live. In fact, one of the most interesting forms of analysis of Barth's work, Barth's relationship to radical politics, enables us to appreciate how encultured Barth's theological thinking is. Marquardt might have over-stretched the early work of Barth in suggesting its affinities with the writings of Lenin, but nevertheless he, and more recently Tim Gorringe (who has compared Barth's thinking to Gramsci's), have shown how contextual is Barth's theology.[4] This early dialectical thinking then does not adequately account for what Christians do [*zu tun*] while too quickly prescribing what they should do. This is interesting because Barth's approach to dialectics in the first edition of *Romans* – whilst emphasizing *Krisis* and *Diakrisis* – is much more Hegelian. That is, it is a dialectic between the Word and the world which operates through the processes of encounter and sublation of the world. It is, then, committed to the historical and the unfolding of that history through what people do [*zu tun*]. Michael Beintker observes Barth's concern with dynamics, growth, and movement in the earlier text and his emphasis on thinking as always in flight. He concludes: 'the dialectic of the first edition of Romans is very close to the massive movement of thought which is Hegelian philosophy'(Beinkter, 1987, 113).[5]

In the second edition of *Romans*, the deepening emphasis upon what Michael Beintker calls the 'the utterly contradictory complexity of profane worldiness' means that 'theology cannot certainly isolate the complexity of profane worldiness from the relationship between God and man' (Beinkter, 1987, 58–9).[6] Dialectical theology (Barth's *Realdialektik*) as 'total contradiction' [*wiederspruchvollen*] submerges incommensurability into theological mystery and weds theological mystery to a highly voluntarist notion of God. The inadequacy of the dialectic, then, arises because Barth needs to give more nuanced accounts of history, agency, and power such that he can reflect more upon the method of his own discourse. He needs to think through the relationship between dialectic as *Denkform* and the noetic and 'ontological connexion between Christ and creation' (*CD*, III.1, 51) – the dialectics of salvation. He needs to negotiate dialectic as *widerspruchvollen Komplexität* with dialectic as process. He needs to wrestle not only with Kierkegaard but with Hegel.[7] Beintker, with respect to examining Barth's dialectic in the second edition of *Romans* and noting the 'not uncomplicated relationship between Barth and Hegel', points to 'a structural relationship between Hegel and Barth with respect to synthesis as a factual origin and end [*als Ur- und Ziel-datum*].' (Beintker, 1987, 72).[8] But this 'structural resemblance' cannot be developed until Barth reconsiders the time and eternity paradox in terms of a lesson Overbeck taught him concerning the operation of *Urgeschichte*. For as Robert E. Hood, observed, for Overbeck the '*Urgeschichte* is the *telos* toward which all history is moving; yet, it is not an abstraction from history' (Hood, 1985, 10). Barth will only be able to begin this reconsideration when he develops his doctrines of the Trinitarian God, creation and reconciliation. As we will see, this will lead to a critical interplay between the dialectical strategy in the first edition of *Romans* and the dialectical strategy in the second.

By the time we come to the introduction to the *Church Dogmatics*, a more adequate dialectic is evident. Here Barth's sharp certainties and clear-cut distinctions are always intentionally compromised by his recognition of the impossibility, and yet necessity, of the theological task itself. He proceeds by identifying clear loci – the Church, on the one hand, unbelief, paganism, heathenism, on the other. But then he qualifies the Church by speaking of the Roman Catholic, Evangelical and Protestant Modernist struggles to be the Church: 'the Church must wrestle with heresy in such a way that it may be itself the Church. And heresy must attack the Church because it is not sufficiently or truly Church' (*CD*, I.1, 33). Faith and the Church are located within this paradoxical struggle that constitutes Barth's dialectical method. They are not then objects as such, nor can they therefore be identified as such. They are positions under constant negotiation; positions articulated only having embarked on the way of the theological enquiry, and, even then, 'We have to state quite definitely that our own under-standing of the being of the Church is in no sense the only one' (*CD*, I.1, 32). Those little words 'quite definitely' betray much – a polemic conducted with respect to both Roman Catholicism and Protestant Modernism in which Barth is 'quite definite' both with respect to his dogmatic certainties (about apologetics) and his uncertainties (the 'intractability of faith' whereby 'divine certainty cannot become human security' (*CD*, I.1, 12)).

The same dual strategy is evident with respect to his other, determinative loci – unbelief. His claim that Christian dog-matics 'speak in the antithesis of faith to unbelief' (*CD*, I.1, 30) marks a precise border between belief in God and godlessness. It is a border separating theology as a science from the other secular sciences; a border maintained through the lack of any 'ground of common presuppositions' (*CD*, I.1, 31) – hence the impossibility of apologetics. But then there are degrees of this unbelief, since there are other accounts of the faith 'in which we hear unbelief express itself' (*CD*, I.1, 31), and Barth ends the opening section on 'The Task of Dogmatics' by claiming that any success for this work is only possible 'on the basis of divine correspondence to this human attitude: "Lord, I believe; help thou my unbelief"' (*CD*, I.1, 24). So when does unbelief become 'pure unbelief'? And since the negotiations to under-stand the faith constitute an ongoing wrestling with possible tragic consequences, when is faith ever without unbelief?

So what happens to the coherence of Barth's understanding of apologetics if the criteria governing that understanding are both identified and qualified and are stated quite definitely with respect to both their identification and qualification? Who identifies the presuppositions that radically distinguish the grounds of difference between the task of theology and the tasks of other sciences? Who judges when the event of faith has taken place? Does this event of faith proffer a 'pure faith' unmixed with unbelief? How are the degrees of faith and unbelief calibrated? Who discerns when theological discourse has been 'empowered and blessed by God'? The Church? Which Church? The contested and contestable Church?

We can confront the problems here from another direction. We can ask why it is that, although theology is human words answering to and working within the operation of the Word of God, there can be no 'human security' in the knowledge of God. Why must theology always be procedural, or 'on its way'? Why is it that 'We always seems to be handling this intractable object with inadequate means' (*CD*, I.1, 23)? For Barth, there are four aspects implicated in any answer to these questions. The first two are theological aspects, and the second two are anthropological aspects. First, there is the nature of the difference and the divide between the gracious addresses of God in Jesus Christ to human beings. Second, there is the operation of 'the free grace of God which may at any time be given or refused' (*CD*, I.1, 18); a freedom whose logic lies in the depth of God's self. Third, there is, from the human perspective, the need to speak in and from faith: 'the presupposition of an anthropological *prius* of faith' (*CD*, I.1, 39). The reception and operation of this faith is manifestly associated with the two theological aspects treated above. But, even so, this mimetic activity of human beings, the 'Christian utterance', the 'humanly speaking' which constitutes 'the work of human knowledge' (*CD*, I.1, 15) is an 'act of human appropriation'. And this appropriation of the Word in human words is constantly in question because it 'is by nature fallible and therefore stands in need of criticism, or correction, of critical amendment and repetition' (*CD*, I.1, 14). This fallibility in appropriation and representation – for there do seem two acts for Barth, human speaking and the act of appropriation – is related to the fallen, sinful nature of being human. This fallenness is the fourth of the aspects implicated in any answer to questions concerning theology's self-reflexive process, inadequate means and partial delivery of truth.

What these aspects assume about theology is three-fold. The first assumption is that there is a pure, ahistorical truth – associated with the Word – that is being pursued through the contingencies and vicissitudes of historical Christian living and thinking. The second one is that there are better (and therefore worse) appropriations of this truth, the measurement of which is again ahistorical: Anselm is a high point, also Luther; Aquinas is a lower point, also Schleiermacher. Thirdly, it is assumed that obedience to the Word, if followed through by all Christians, would lead to a consensus and agreement on all matters of doctrine – would lead, that is, to a Church dogmatics that all Christians could subscribe to whatever their time, place, race or gender.

Putting to one side the voluntarist account of God as the agent of grace, which seems to render all events of grace arbitrary interruptions into creaturely existence,[9] and putting aside the way in which this characterization of both God and God's agency constructs another clear-cut and categorical distinction between God and godlessness, God's self-presence and God's utter absence in creation; putting aside, then, two major theological reservations about this account of God *vis-à-vis* the world, Barth is emphatic that the realm in which theological enquiry is either blessed or idle speculation is discursive. It reduces down to 'Christian speech [that] must be tested by its conformity to Christ. This conformity is never clear and unambiguous' (*CD*, I.1, 13). So that which dogmatics investigates is nothing other than 'Christian utterance' (*CD*, I.1, 12).[10]

Barth points out that this attention paid to Christian utterance by dogmatics renders theological enquiry a 'self-enclosed circle' of concern (*CD*, I.1, 42), and it is the self-enclosed nature of this concern which means that theology takes itself, rather than *extra ecclesia* concerns, seriously. Dogmatics cannot be anything other than unintentionally apologetic because of the self-enclosure of Christian utterance. The moment it steps out of this enclosure to speak to those without faith it adopts alien categories. 'Apologetics is an attempt to show by means of thought and speech that the determining principles of philosophy and of historical and natural research at some given point in time certainly do not preclude, even if they do not directly require, the tenets of theology' (Barth, 2001, 425–6). But it is at this point that a critical intervention can be made. Discourse is recognized as fundamental. It defines the faithfulness of dogmatics and the unfaithfulness of apologetics, while betraying the incomplete and fallible nature of all dogmatic enquiry. But who can police the boundaries of any discourse, Christian or otherwise? Put more precisely, who can ensure the self-enclosure when the constitution of that enclosure is a question of language and representation? Does the belief in the self-enclosure of certain linguistic practices not presuppose the distinct separation of different discourses and forms of reason? Barth points to as much when he declares: 'There has never been a *philosophia christiana*, for if it was *philosophia* it was not *christiana*, and if it was *christiana* it was not *philosophia*' (*CD*, I.1, 6). Theological discourse or Christian thinking is rendered utterly distinct from philosophical discourse, historical discourse or scientific discourses of various kinds. But who defines and maintains the autonomy of these discourses? Doesn't Barth's description of research conducted on the basis of 'determining principles' sound like the academic rationale for distinct and jealously guarded faculty boundaries in a post-Berlin university? For – and this is the main point I wish to make here – if discourses are not bounded, if discourses exceed institutional, contested and contestable framings then an apologetics can proceed without the theologian *necessarily* renouncing his or her 'theological function.' Recently, Kathryn Tanner, in a critical discussion of postliberalism's Barthian account of the autonomy of discrete language games (of which Christianity would be one), has observed that contemporary cultural anthropology argues strongly against the corollary of this thesis which suggests that 'Christians have a self-sustaining society and culture of their own, which can be marked off rather sharply from others' (Tanner, 1997, 96).[11] Christian utterance is constructed out of the cultural materials at hand. It is not homogenous but always hybrid, improvised and implicated in networks of association which exceed various forms of institutional, individual or sectarian policing. Furthermore, since Christians are also members of other associations, networks and institutions, what is both internal and external to Christian identity (and its continuing formation) is fluid.

What is significant is that in the very performance of his dialectic, the very process of the realization of his thoughts, Barth reweaves what he has already woven in a manner that suggests a negotiation with a thesis he has already negated. And it is this aspect of his dialectic that I wish to examine with respect to Hegel. For, while Barth suggests Christianity is self-defining and must be so in order to protect itself from the corrupting external influences of secular society, he himself reveals how interdependent Christian utterance is upon the discourses of other disciplines. His own writing demonstrates how vocabularies and categories are not discrete and how Christianity always defines itself in terms of that to which it allies itself or from which it distinguishes itself. In defining the dogmatic task Barth employs categories like 'knowledge', 'consciousness', 'conception', 'understanding', 'formal' and 'ontological-ontic'; he refers continually (though admittedly not depending upon their investigations) to Plato, Aristotle, Descartes, Kant and Heidegger; he situates his task with respect to the older Protestant orthodoxy, to 'historical development of at least the last two or three hundred years' (*CD*, I.1, 9) and to the mediaeval writings of Anselm, Bonaventura and Aquinas; he speaks of 'other sciences' social, psychological and natural. Barth can then only proceed to define his particular form of Protestantism upon the basis of shared vocabularies, categories and reference points that stand 'outside' and other to his thesis. The very German he writes, while translating these other discourses into his own Christian thesis, is working across other languages like Greek and Latin. His is not a 'self-enclosed' discursive reflection; and neither *can* Christian theology or Christian living be self-enclosed. As the dialectic issues from an understanding of the ongoing and yet to be perfected Word and work of God in the act of reconciling the world to Himself, so Christian theology can neither be completely systematized nor, *a priori*, stake out the limits of what is in and what is outside Christ. Theology *is* a cultural activity;

the dialectic it is implicated in is, simultaneously, transhistorical, historical and material. And here again, Barth encounters Hegel.

It is, I suggest, Hegel more than Schleiermacher who lies behind Barth's categorical assertion that 'There has never been a *philosophia christiana*, for if it was *philosophia* it was not *christiana*, and if it was *christiana* it was not *philosophia*.' For it is Hegel who poses the challenge of the relationship between philosophy and theology by conflating the dialectic of reason with Trinitarian procession. Thus it followed that 'everything that seems to give theology its particular splendour and special dignity appears to be looked after and honoured by this philosophy in a way comparably better than that achieved by the theologians themselves' (Barth, 2001, 382).[12] The language of appearance is telling here. Barth (and a number of Hegel scholars before and after him) is not quite certain where Hegel – the orthodox Lutheran – falls into heterodoxy. But, Barth wishes nevertheless to point out that Hegel's work consummates the Prometheanism of human confidence in the act of thinking, in the Enlightenment categories such as mind, idea, concept and reason – something that he views as inimical both to dogmatics and the dialectical encounter with the Word of God which is the contents of dogmatics. It is Hegel then who proclaims the possibility of a *philosophia christiana* – and Aquinas, whom Barth consistently brackets with Hegel. His reading of Aquinas is wrong and his persistent reading of Hegel's dialectical method as 'thesis, antithesis and synthesis', with an emphasis upon consummation of the absolute, owes more to left-wing Hegelians after Hegel (Strauss and Marx, in particular) than Hegel himself.[13]

Nevertheless, his observation that, for Hegel, 'God is only God in his divine action, revelation, creation, reconciliation, redemption; as an absolute act, *actus purus*' demonstrates how close Hegel (and Aquinas) is to Barth (Barth, 2001, 385). And, characteristically, in Barth's short but excellent analysis of Hegel in *Protestant Theology in the Nineteenth Century,* the condemnation of the univocity of *Geist* and reason that reveals Hegel's inability to take seriously either sin or God's freedom with respect to confronting human beings in their sin is offset by a recognition of the unfulfilled and 'great promise' in Hegel's work (Barth, 2001, 407). 'Doubtless, theology could and can learn something from Hegel as well. It looks as if theology had neglected something here, and certainly it has no occasion to assume an attitude of alarm and hostility to any renaissance of Hegel that might come about' (Barth, 2001, 403). When we examine what it is that remains promising for Barth in Hegel it is in fact the Trinitarian-informed reflexivity of his dialectic. Though Barth chides him for his unsatisfactory doctrine of the Trinity, he applauds Hegel's reminder 'of the possibility that the truth might be history' and that theology's knowledge 'was only possible in the form of a strict obedience to the self-movement of truth, and therefore as a knowledge which was itself moved' (Barth, 2001, 401–2). Furthermore, in Hegel's commitment to theology as a material practice participating in the unfolding of a history of God's own self-unveiling, theology is reminded 'of the contradictory nature of its own knowledge'. For 'Hegel with his concept of mind, must wittingly, or unwittingly have been thinking of the Creator of heaven and earth, the Lord over nature and spirit, precisely by virtue of the unity and opposition of *dictum* and *contra-dictum*, in which Hegel had the spirit conceiving itself and being real' (Barth, 2001, 402).

There are three things, then, that Barth recognizes of theological value in Hegel: history as a material process informed by God; theology as a discursive practice participating in what he will elsewhere conceive as 'The covenant of grace [a]s *the* theme of history' (*CD*, III.1, 60); and the need for theology to be reflexive about that practice because the words and works of human beings can never be identical to the unveiling of God.

The question remains as to the extent to which Barth integrated these insights into his own theological thinking – he had certainly not done so when the lecture on Hegel was given in the early 1930s. But there is a hint of what Barth will develop as he and the Christian Church stood in the twilight of a global history of world-occurrence. For in what appears almost to be an aside in the Introduction to the *Church Dogmatics*, he observes: 'The separate existence of theology signifies the

emergency measure on which the Church has had to resolve in
view of the actual refusal of the other sciences in this respect'
(*CD*, I.1, 7). The observation points to not a pragmatism but the
temporal specificity about theology's task. Its 'separate existence' is a response to a culture and a historical moment when
the theological is despised.[14] As with his view of discrete discourses for discrete disciplines, the dogmatic in opposition to
the apologetic task of theology becomes a cultural production
(and a cultural producer in its own right); one that *necessarily*,
on Barth's own axioms, 'stands in need of criticism, or correction, of critical amendment and repetition.' The necessity
comes about when Christian theology and therefore the task of
the Christian theologian is elsewhere implicated in a different
kind of cultural productivity. By the end of the Second World
War – when Barth was completing the opening volume of his
doctrine of creation – history, the theological practice of participating in that history and the need to consider more carefully that biblical witnesses speak as men, and not as angels or
gods' (*CD*, III.1, 93), give rise to a different reflection and a new
kind of dialectic.

Thus we have to reckon on their part with all kinds of human
factors, with their individual and general capacities of perception and expression, with their personal views and style, as
determined by age and environment, and of course with the
limitations and deficiencies of these conditioning factors – in
this case the limitations of their imagination (*CD*, III.1, 93).

Barth is specifically examining the creation stories as the
Word of God, but in his development of the category of 'saga'
and his recognition of the different genres of Biblical writing,
he speaks more generally of Biblical witness. The commitment
to a God who does not transcend history but informs it at every
point, to an account of eternity as the origin and telos of the
history, not its erasure, leads to an understanding of Biblical
discourse as culturally and psychologically 'determined'. I
am not going to follow the psychological trajectory of Barth's
thinking as such, but shall only comment that 'personal views',
expression and style – and some would even say, individual
levels and direction of perception – cannot be divorced from

the 'conditioning factors' of 'age and environment'. But in my concern to assess the possibility for apologetics that begin from a Christian theological standpoint, this recognition of the cultural embeddedness of Biblical discourse is an important move towards seeing that theological discourse cannot be simply self-referring and 'overheard' by other publics. Biblical witness borrows materials and forms of representation and refigures them for its own purposes. The accounts it furnishes of things prehistorical or historical involve cultural negotiations, 'textual relationships' (*CD*, III.1, 87) and human knowing that 'is not exhausted by the ability to perceive and comprehend' (*CD*, III.1, 91). Barth even employs Schleiermacher's hermeneutical category of 'divination' to speak of the way the writer has to divine the vision of the true historical emergence (the operation of God in creation) that preceded the 'historical' events so cherished by professional historians and historicism. The questions of 'depiction and narration' issue not from discussing the abstractions of time and eternity, but from the covenant of grace that *is* the theme of God's history. Time is in God, and so though the truth of God's Word is eternal, it is also highly specific. 'Creation is not a timeless truth … there are no timeless truths; truth has a concretely temporal character' (*CD*, III.1, 60).

Of course, Barth's attention here is to biblical witness and biblical writing. But since this witness and writing must be the source and prototype for all Christian witness and writing, then, although Barth says little about the cultural and historical embeddedness of his own discourse, this must follow. In fact, again almost as an aside, he writes: 'concerning the ground and being of man and his world, we are referred to our own metaphysical and scientific genius, or to our own powers in the construction of myth or saga' (*CD*, III.1, 61). Christian theology tells God's story in the place any theologian finds himself or herself situated. Such story-telling cannot but rehearse and refigure the language, ideologies, cultural assumptions, fears, guilts and dreams of its times. The theologian attempts to read the signs of those times in terms of the continuing covenant of grace, but in reading those signs cultural negotiations are set in operation. Theological discourse is involved in the wider cultural dissemination and exchange of signs. Other people will be telling the story of what is from where they are and possibly using some of the same materials and reference points. And while Christian theology (like the Biblical witnesses) speaks of the 'genuinely historical' (*CD*, III.1, 66) relationship between God and human beings – such that cultural relativism is not a question raised – Christian theology cannot transcend the historical and cultural determination and conditions. If it cannot transcend them then it equally cannot distil for itself some purely theological discourse.

Christian theology is then implicated in cultural negotiations, and to that extent is engaged in an ongoing apologetics. Barth, it seems, moves towards an integration of what Beintker (after Henning Schroer) termed the 'complementary' and 'supplementary' of paradox. Barth forges a theological method that brings together, in a creative tension, the synchronic dialectic of Kierkegaard's 'infinite qualitative difference' with the diachronic dialectic of Hegel's 'possibility that the truth might be history' and that theology's knowledge 'was only possible in the form of a strict obedience to the self-movement of truth, and therefore as a knowledge which was itself moved'. The synchronic and the diachronic can supplement each other in the work of the theologian with respect to the world.

Allow me now to pursue this further by referring back to the third of Barth's affirmations about Hegel's project: the need for theology to be reflexive about that practice because the words and works of human beings can never be identical to the unveiling of God. For Beintker characterizes the 'complementary' use of paradox as involving an asymmetrical relationship between thesis and antithesis, such that the reconciliation or sublation proceeds through the absorption of the latter by the former. This is parallel to the asymmetrical relation in Hegel's thinking between the in-itself and the for-itself such that, in the dialectical process of being with oneself in an other then the other is integrated into one's own projects. In this way the other fulfils and perfects the same; it becomes part of the free activity of the subject. Barth's description of the dialectic of sexual difference bears something of this Hegelian model (see Ward, 2000, 183–202). But since theology moves between Christ's Word and a cultural situation in which 'There are no forms, events or relationships ... unmistakeably confused by man in which the goodness of what God has created is not also effective and visible, the only question being how this is so' (*CD*, IV.3, 698) – then it has no unqualified access to that asymmetrical relationship. And, if this is so, it may not so easily take up the 'complementary' use of paradox that judges the other only to have value with respect to the same. It cannot judge and subjugate the world to its own discourse. For theology cannot leave out the possibility that in this cultural other God is at work, and engagement with this other may mean it is not subordinated but allowed to challenge radically the theological project. Cultural negotiation must run such a risk – the risk of being disrupted. The 'supplementary' use of paradox allows for what George Hunsinger has recently termed 'disruptive grace' (Hunsinger, 2000). But the 'supplementary' use of paradox is also asymmetrical, and it is at this point that the theologian needs to cultivate a healthy agnosticism with respect to what he or she knows. Space must be allowed, on the basis of what theology understands about itself and the God with whom it has to do, for the other to speak. This enables the cultural engagement of Christian apologetics to be a negotiated engagement.

The last reference to Hegel, whose dialectic I am suggesting opens Barth's theology to the possibility of apologetics as Christian cultural negotiation, comes in *Church Dogmatics* IV.3.2 and the development of his doctrine of reconciliation. Here Barth's dialectical structure is firmly in place in a discussion of the interface between *Hominum confusione et Dei providentia* in the call of Christ to all humanity. But he seeks a third way beyond the antithesis, and this is where he introduces Hegel. Again, it is the Hegel of the thesis–antithesis–synthesis – Hegel reduced to a formula that can then be haughtily dismissed. What Barth wishes to avoid is a *tertium quid.* So what he offers 'the Christian community as *it is required* to go beyond that twofold view' (emphasis mine) is the 'reality and

truth of the grace of God addressed to the world in Jesus Christ'
(*CD*, IV.3.2, 706). What this amounts to is that the Christian
community is enjoined to speak to the world about Jesus
Christ while recognizing that, on the one hand, Jesus Christ
'is not a concept which man can think out for himself, which
he can define with more or less precision, and with the help of
which he can then display his mastery over … this problem of
this antithesis' (*CD*, IV.3.2, 706); and, on the other hand, understanding that 'We think and speak like poor heathen, no matter
how earnestly we may imagine that we think and speak of it
[the grace of God addressed to the world in Jesus Christ]' (*CD*,
IV.3.2, 707). Which leaves us where exactly? With the knowledge
of the *diastasis*, concerning which there is no 'real synthesis',
and yet … the fallible Christian community as the bearer of
and the witness to a better hope testifies to the work and Word
of God as a 'new thing in relation to that contradiction' (*CD*,
IV.3.2, 708). It not only testifies but, in testifying, seeks to participate in the unfolding of that new world; and so it attempts
to perform and produce that 'new thing'. To take this further,
its practice of transformative hope, executed in the name of
Christ, is disseminated through the world because the living
community of the Church is implicated in other 'communities' and practices. Those characterized as the community
of the Church participate in the operations of other desires
that are not *prima facie* theological but only *de jure* theological because Jesus Christ is both the 'loftiest, most luminous
transcendence' and 'heard in the deepest, darkest immanence'
(Barth, 1961, 46). These members as the community of the
Church are also members of other forms of fellowship, other
bodies – industrial, commercial, agricultural, political, sport-
ing, domestic. Barth too was a member of a political party. To
return to a moment mentioned earlier in the first editions of
Romans, it is because Christians are involved in 'monarchism,
capitalism, militarism, patriotism and liberalism', among other
things (things working against the hegemony of such ideologies) that the work and words of the living community extend
out into the 'deepest, darkest immanence' in their testimony
to and performance of a 'new thing'. This is movement in,

through and beyond the Church, in through and beyond the Church's endless cultural negotiations. It is not a dialectic of progress or growth, because it moves between mysteries and confusion, but it is nevertheless teleologically driven. It is then a positive dialectic tracing and performing of what Hegel called 'the march of God in the world' (Hegel, 1991, 279). We may not like Hegel's metaphor, but I suggest that upon this basis an apologetics, no longer saddled with defining itself against *Kulturprotestantismus*, can proceed: reading and producing the signs of the times and negotiating a role in defining public truth; taking its own historical and cultural embeddedness with all theological seriousness.

Graham Ward is professor of contextual theology and ethics at the University of Manchester.

WORKS CITED

Barth, K. (1956–1975) *Church Dogmatics*, 14 volumes, Edinburgh: T&T Clark.

Barth, K. (1961), *The Humanity of God*, London: Collins.

Barth, K. (1963), *Der Romerbrief*, 1st edn, Zurich: EVZ-Verlag.

Barth, K. (1968), 'Church and State', in *Community, State and Church*, trans. A. M. Hall *et al.*, Gloucester, Mass.: Peter Smith.

Barth, K. (1990), *The Göttingen Dogmatics: Instruction in the Christian Religion*, I, trans. Geoffrey W. Bromiley, Grand Rapids: William B. Eerdmans.

Barth, K. (2001), *Protestant Theology in the Nineteenth Century*, tr. Brian Cozens and John Bowden, London: SCM.

Beinkter, M. (1987), *Die Dialektik in der 'dialektischen Theologie' Karl Barths*, Munich: Ch. Kaiser Verlag.

Edwards, M., Goodman, M., and Price, S. (eds) (1999), *Apologetics in the Roman Empire: Pagans, Jews, and Christians*, Oxford: Oxford University Press.

Gorringe, T. (1999), *Karl Barth: Against Hegemony*, Oxford: Oxford University Press.

Hegel, G. W. F. (1991), *Elements of the Philosophy of Right*, trans. H. B. Nisbet, Cambridge: Cambridge University Press.

Hood, R. E. (1985), *Contemporary Political Order and Christ: Karl Barth's Christology and Political Praxis*, Allison Park: Pickwick Publications.

Hunsinger, G. (2000), *Disruptive Grace: Studies in the Theology of Karl Barth*, Grand Rapids: William B. Eerdmans.

Hunsinger, G. (ed.) (1976), *Karl Barth and Radical Politics*, Philadelphia: Westminster.

Lakeland, P. (1982), *The Politics of Salvation: The Hegelian Idea of the State*, Albany: SUNY.

McCormack, B. (1995), *Karl Barth's Critically Realistic Dialectical Theology: Its Genesis and Development 1909–1936*, Oxford: Oxford University Press.

Marquardt, F.-W. (1972), *Theologie und Socialismus: Das Beispiel Karl Barths*, Munich: Grunewald.

Niebuhr, H. R. (1951), *Christ and Culture*, New York: Harper & Row.

Shanks, A. (1991), *Hegel's Political Theology*, Cambridge: Cambridge University Press.

Tanner, K. (1997), *Theories of Culture: A New Agenda for Theology*, Minneapolis: Fortress Press.

Ward, G. (2000), *Cities of God*, London: Routledge.

Wood, A. (1991), 'Introduction', in G. W. F. Hegel, *Elements of the Philosophy of Right*, trans. H. B. Nisbet, Cambridge: Cambridge University Press.

NOTES

1   I am aware by giving emphasis to the church as the body of Christ and the role of the sacraments in creating, sustaining and fostering the growth of that body that these are more Catholic elements than Barth would have espoused. But I am not trying to reproduce Barth's theology in this essay. Rather I wish to engage it in developing a theological project with respect to the Christian faith today. The Church is not today where Barth once was.

2   It needs to be pointed out that, on the basis of his exposure to and researches in nineteenth-century German theology and his in-depth analysis of Schleiermacher's work during his Göttingen employment, Barth conflates 'apologetics' with '*Kulturprotestantismus*'. For an understanding of theologically driven apologetics, see Edwards (1999).

3   I am saying nothing here that Barth did not admit, almost forty years later, in his 1956 address 'The Humanity of God'. See Barth (1961), 37–65.

4   See Marquardt (1972) and Gorringe (1999). Of course, the work of George Hunsinger's edited volume (1976) and also Bruce McCormack's (1995) should be added here.

5   '*Damit ist die Dialektik von Römer I als bewegungsmassiges Denken derjenigen Hegelscher Philosophie sehr nahe*'.

6   '*widerspruchsvollen Komplexität profaner Weltlichkeit*' [means that] '*Der Theologie kann allerdings die Komplexität profaner Weltlichkeit*

nicht von der Beziehung zwischen Gott und Mensch isolierien.' Beintker distinguishes this form of dialectic from the form in the first edition of *Romans* by differentiating between the employment of 'complementary' and 'supplementary' paradoxes. In the complementary *Paradoxdialektik* an asymmetrical relationship holds between the thesis and the antithesis, but (to use the Hegelian term) the thesis can sublate the antithesis and hence move forward. With the supplementary employment of paradox no movement is possible because the two terms are radically antithetical to each other.

7 As several commentators have pointed out (including Barth himself), beyond appreciating the theological importance of concepts such as paradox, either/or, the moment, difference, and fear and trembling, Barth never really undertook a thorough study and analysis of dialectic. See Beintker, 230–8. It is surprising that, to my knowledge, only in the chapter on Hegel in *Protestant Theology in the Nineteenth Century* does Barth really engage with Hegel's thinking. The early distinction he makes between Hegel's *Dialektik* and Kierkegaard's *Realdialektik* in *The Göttingen Dogmatics* goes unelaborated (Barth, 1990, 77). Later, in the *Church Dogmatics* considering Hegel's dominance in German thinking with respect to construals of history, reconciliation and community, he appears mainly as a name in a list of other names. There is neither refutation nor quotation of Hegel in the section almost screaming for comparative and penetrating analysis – III.1, 'Creation, History and Creation History'. We will come to the reference in IV.3, 'The Holy Spirit and the Sending of the Christian Community' later.

8 '*eine Strukturverwandtschaft zwischen Hegel und Barth im Blick auf das Synthetische als Ur- and Zieldatum.'*

9 I put 'seems' because the critics of Barth on this very point may have missed something. There is a question here as to whether the events of God's grace are arbitrary and interruptive only from the human perspective. That is, is there a continuum of activity as far as God is concerned with respect to creation such that the veiling and unveiling of God's self is what human beings in their darkened and unredeemed state discern? Or is creation so wholly other from God, not only in its fallenness – which can only be contingent with respect to the determination of divine salvation – but in its essence, such that any divine activity with respect to creation enters it from an ontologically distinct and prior exteriority? When Barth is developing his doctrine of creation, based upon his *analogia relationis*, he is emphatic that time and creation are not in contradiction to the eternal Godhead but 'in Him'.

10 Of course this idea of the dogmatic task as investigating what Christians say and do developed into postliberalism's distinction between first- and second-order discourses. The assumed role of the dogmatician is then both diagnositic (with respect to its investigation into Christian utterance) and regulative (with respect to bring-

ing that utterance into a better understanding of its relation to the Word). It is not only doubtful that such a distinction can be made between practice and theory, it is not only questionable whether the distinction should be made (which privileges academic theologians, or at least sets them as a class apart from others by reinforcing a dualism between practical and dogmatic theology), it is manifest from Barth's own writings how little account is given of the Christian utterances (apart from those of other academic theologians). We gain little insight into the actual everyday living of this church with respect to whom and for whom Barth is writing his dogmatics. The question of authority – for whom is this task being undertaken, with what jurisdiction and to whom is it addressed? – hollows Barth's text.

11 Interestingly, while the critique of postliberalism is unabated, all Tanner's references to Barth – the theological spinal chord of postliberalism – are uncritical and affirmative.

12 This repeats his conclusion about Hegel's speculative trinity in *The Göttingen Dogmatics*, where he observes Hegel's 'replacement of the Christian trinity by a logical and metaphysical Trinity and by the relegation of the Christian Trinity to the sphere of naïve, symbolical, and inadequate conceptions' (Barth, 1990, 105). But nothing positive about Hegel's thinking is said in this earlier work. By the time the lectures on the history of nineteenth-century Protestant theology were given in their last form (Winter 1932–33), Barth is much more appreciative of Hegel's potential.

13 Elsewhere Barth makes evident that he interpreted the relationship in Hegel's thought between *Sittlichkeit* and *Staat* as the deification of German nationalism that courted the hubris leading to the betrayals by the theological establishment in the First World War. This too is a wrong reading of Hegel's *Elements of the Philosophy of Right*. See Wood, 1991; Lakeland, 1982; Shanks, 1991; Ward, 2000, 137–46. Hegel would in fact concur with Barth's own judgement (albeit with a different doctrine of the Trinity): 'the State as such belongs originally and ultimately to Jesus Christ' (Barth, 1968, 118).

14 In his study *Christ and Culture*, H. Richard Niebuhr points out the association between the Christian response to the cultural and the cultural response to Christianity. He does not develop this insight to any depth, but, significantly, the first of his five models for the 'enduring problem' of Christian theology with respect to its cultural context, Christ against culture, first arises because of the persecution of the church. This defines the Church as a new creation in Christ totally separate from what Barth called 'world-occurrences', and a Christology emphasising Christ as King, Lord, and Lawgiver. See, Niebuhr, 1951, 45–115.

Reading the Bible Theologically:
Text, Church and Life

EDMUND NEWEY

Recent scholarly writing on biblical exegesis has shown an increasing interest in patristic and mediaeval models of 'pre-critical' exegesis. This enthusiasm has sprung largely from a frustration with the tendency of biblical criticism to concern itself either with purely textual issues (redactional, source-critical and so on), or with questions of the community and cultural background from which the books of the Bible have arisen.[1] The various forms of 'pre-critical' exegesis seek, rather, to emphasize the continuity between the different strands and traditions in the Bible (as with Brevard Child's 'canonical criticism') or to overcome the distinctions between areas of academic study, such as theology, ethics and biblical studies, which have been increasingly sharply demarcated in the modern era. Bible and Church, theology and life are seen as a whole, not in isolation.

There are of course dangers with such an approach. Is it a return to the past, an attempt to bury one's head in the sand and to disregard the critical faculties which are an essential part of our present day view of the world? Does it also, at least in certain forms, run the risk of smoothing over those aspects of the text of which modern feminist and liberationist perspectives have taught us to be suspicious? These are real questions, yet it is increasingly clear, as Hauerwas, Williams and Fowl among many others observe, that without an attempt to overcome the 'compartmentalisation' of scholarly disciplines, there is little possibility of coming to a proper understanding of the way the Bible relates to ethical living in the present.[2]

A recent university examination question provides a nice illustration of the shape of this modern predicament. Ordinands were asked: 'Is it possible to distinguish "timeless truths" from "culturally conditioned elements" when we come to use the Bible in ethics?' The difficulties with this formulation are many. First, in its use of the phrase 'come to use' it conjures up an image of the Bible as a self-contained text to which we turn when confronted with discrete ethical problems. As this article attempts to demonstrate, such a view of the Bible is both peculiarly modern and profoundly misguided. Even the idea of 'using' the Bible is unfortunate, not because the Bible is irrelevant, but because the Bible should be an integral part of our approach to life, informing our whole Christian practice. My second objection to the question concerns its opposition of 'timeless truth' to 'culturally conditioned elements'. The problem here is not with the terms used – clearly the Bible is both timelessly true (is there any other form of truth?) and culturally conditioned (how could it be otherwise?) – but with their opposition. It is in the nature of classical texts, from *The Odyssey* to *Beloved*, that their 'classical' quality resides precisely in the fact that from their specific 'culturally conditioned' origin, they are able to speak truth to their own and subsequent ages as well as to different cultural settings. Their universality arises out of their very particularity. That the Christian faith teaches that the Bible is divinely inspired does not alter this state of affairs. The divine inspiration lies not in the delivery of the Bible as the unsullied word of God, intact and pure, but in the fact that it is a human witness to the loving action of God in the world. In the Bible the human and the divine are mysteriously interwoven, just as they are in the Church and, supremely, in the person of Christ.[3]

These criticisms notwithstanding, it is nonetheless clear that the formulation of the exam question could, at least at first sight, appear unproblematic. The separation between Bible and ethics, between the timeless and the culturally specific, is one that is deeply felt in the modern era. In what follows I shall examine some of the ways in which contemporary theologians are seeking to overcome such dichotomies and to reassert the centrality of theology, not just as an academic discipline, but as a practical way of life appropriate and necessary for all the faithful.

The key figure at the root of such recent reassessments is Karl Barth. His work can be seen as an attempt to rebuild theology as divinely inspired speech about God, in the face of its increasingly anthropological concerns since the Enlightenment. The problems with Barth's approach – chiefly its apparent subsumption of human freedom into God and its over-hasty dismissal of such thinkers as Schleiermacher – are well documented, but his influence on contemporary theology remains vital. Thus the American narrative theologian and ethicist, Stanley Hauerwas, begins a recent article with the following quotation from the *Church Dogmatics* II/2:

> When we speak of ethics, the term cannot include anything more than this confirmation of the truth of the grace of God as it is addressed to man. If dogmatics, if the doctrine of God, is ethics, this means necessarily and decisively that it is the attestation of that divine ethics, the attestation of the good of the command issued to Jesus Christ and fulfilled by Him.[4]

Hauerwas is entirely in agreement with Barth that there can be no ontological or practical independence of ethics from theology or from biblical interpretation, even if they may sometimes be distinguished for purely heuristic purposes. Unlike Barth, however, he has a more positive attitude to the position, usually described as 'natural law', adopted by Thomas Aquinas. This is because Hauerwas believes that natural law has been misunderstood since the Enlightenment as a series of rational derivations of eternal truth from the natural state of the world. In fact, he believes, in the Middle Ages 'natural law was only intelligible as part of divine law as mediated by the Church'.[5] This mediaeval and catholic emphasis on the Church as the context giving order to Christian life is a fundamental part of Hauerwas's strategy, yet it is combined with a Barthian stress on the 'concreteness of God's command as found in Jesus Christ'.[6] By this marriage of the scriptural and the ecclesial, the Protestant and the Catholic, Hauerwas points a way to a new understanding of the coherence of the Christian life beyond the damaging fragmentation of modernity.

For Hauerwas 'the persuasive power of Christian discourse rests upon the indissociable unity of the theological and the ethical aspects of Christian faith'.[7] Stephen Fowl, in his recent book *Engaging Scripture*, develops this perspective in his account of how Christians can relate theologically to Scripture in the contemporary world. He begins by defining two characteristically modern strategies of approach to the Bible by the terms 'determinate' and 'anti-determinate' interpretation. 'Determinate' interpretation views the text as 'a relatively stable element in which an author inserts, hides or dissolves (choose your metaphor) meaning'.[8] Clearly there is disagreement over the means by which we are to rediscover this concealed meaning of the text, but the unifying assumption is that 'matters of doctrine and practice are straightforwardly determined by biblical interpretation and never the other way around'.[9] Anti-determinate interpretation, by contrast, is a reaction against this stress on stability and unity of meaning. It emphasizes the relativity of meaning and the inevitable influence of context on both the composition and the reading of the text. Even the notion of the text itself is brought into doubt by 'anti-determinate' movements such as deconstructionism, which view language as an endless play of signifiers with no attachment to anything specifically signified.

The purpose of Fowl's definition of these two terms is to point out that modern approaches to a text, and to the biblical text in particular, almost invariably adopt one or other of these strategies: either an excessively simplistic, univocal 'determinate' reading or, in direct reaction against it, a pluralistic, relativizing 'anti-determinate' one. In a development of Hauerwas's position, Fowl then advances an alternative approach, which he characterizes under the general term of 'underdetermined interpretation'. He does not claim this as original but finds it in a number of recent attempts to return more closely to premodern patterns of scriptural reading, such as those of Rowan Williams, L.Gregory Jones and Eugene Rogers. Such 'underdetermined' readings place relatively little stress on particular theories of reading, though they may make use of them on an *ad hoc* basis. Instead they seek to emphasize the interdependent nature of the relationship between text and reader. In the case of the Bible this interdependence is most clearly present in the Church as the Body of Christ, to which both the biblical text and its readers belong. This approach is not intended to lead to a new form of ecclesial fundamentalism, however. Rather it sees scriptural interpretation as a practice that both shapes and is shaped by Christian convictions, recognizing 'both the provisionality and plurality of biblical interpretation ... and [being] self-reflexively critical of Christian practice, without practising deconstruction'.[10]

One of the most significant concomitants of such 'under-determined' readings is that the conventional distinctions between theology, exegesis and ethics are relativized. Instead, these supposedly separate areas of research are shown to be intimately inter-related, so that textual interpretation ceases to be an independent exercise divorced from doctrine and from the practice of Christian life. This is in many ways a rediscovery of the patristic and mediaeval perspective on scripture. It involves a reappropriation of the view that doctrinal orthodoxy, rather than being a series of restrictive constraints imposed by a monolithic Church authority, is instead a means of preserving the freedom of the Christian faith. Ecclesial doctrine, in this understanding, operates as a form of regulative grammar, guiding our reading of the Bible, helping to exclude narrowings of the wholeness of the faith and to foster its flourishing. As Rowan Williams observes, 'the history of theology itself, particularly patristic theology, is a history of exegesis (and so its crises are crises for the *principles* of exegesis)'.[11]

As an example of this inter-relation of exegesis, doctrine and ethics, one could cite the christological and Trinitarian debates of the early church. The development of an orthodox position cannot be seen as a simple triumph of truth over error. Rather, orthodox doctrine emerged gradually through the course of the debates. Thus it slowly became clear that the breadth of scriptural witness to the person and work of Christ was best expressed by the declaration that he was consubstantial with God in his divinity and with humankind in his humanity. That terms such as 'consubstantial' are not biblical is only an incidental problem, because the doctrines of the Church seek not to add to scripture but to enable our faithful and truthful reading of it. As the Lutheran scholar David Yeago puts it:

> the Nicene *homoousion* is neither imposed *on* the New Testament texts, nor distantly deduced from the texts, but, rather, describes a pattern of judgements present in the texts, in the texture of scriptural discourse concerning Jesus and the God of Israel.

Ecclesial dogma thus fosters an 'attention (in Athanasius's terms) to the *skopos* and *akolouthia*, the tenor and coherence of the judgements rendered in the texts'.[12]

It is in the application of these disciplines of attentive and vigilant reading of scripture, guided by the Church's doctrinal grammar, that we are able to approach the ethical dilemmas of life in a scripturally informed way. Thus Nicholas Lash, commenting on Acts 6:4 reminds us that we are not to dissociate 'meaning from feeding, conversing from caring, announcing from enacting'.[13] Seen in this light the Bible is not a textbook to be consulted for ethical guidance, nor is Church doctrine a series of constrictive impositions. Rather the two work together to guide and shape our Christian practice, to aid us to speak truthfully of, and live faithfully to, God.

Fowl's approach is particularly illuminating here, as it illustrates the extent to which the character of the interpreter has a bearing on the nature of her interpretation of scripture. Making use of the perspectives of Alasdair MacIntyre and Stanley Hauerwas on the importance of the virtues in Christian ethical life, he shows how vital it is that the Church enable its members to read the Bible virtuously. To do so is not merely a human work but is part of the action of the Holy Spirit in the Church, after the example of the scriptural reading of the early Church: 'If Christians are to learn to read like Paul (among others), both reading the Spirit and reading with the Spirit, then the character of the interpreter will also become a factor in the offering, hearing and enacting of their interpretations'.[14]

Thus the reading of scripture is not an isolated exercise, done in private, but something that happens in the Church community, which should train and equip its members to read lovingly, and which should allow for mutual criticism in a spirit of charity (which is also the work of the Holy Spirit in us). Such an approach allows for disagreement and difference, because it is aware of the complexity and variety of particular human responses to the word of God, yet it encourages discussion and the search for enlightenment by the sharing of disparate interpretations: 'Interpretative charity ... presumes that by illuminating points of agreement and by minimizing ascriptions of irrationality one can better account for the words and deeds of others, not that one has to agree with them'.[15] Lash draws out this point further by relating it to sacramental theology, seeing the Eucharist as a 'performance of the biblical text', which 'to be true ... must be not only "true to life" but "true to his [Jesus's] life"; and not only "true to his life", but "true to God".'[16] The life of the Christian, then, is to be seen as a performance of the scriptures, seeking always to remain faithful to the triune God, to whose life they point:

> If the NT texts are to express that which Christian faith declares them capable of expressing, the quality of our *humanity* will be the criterion of the adequacy of our performance. And yet this criterion is, in the last resort, hidden from us in the mystery of God whose meaning for [humanity] we are bidden to enact.[17]

In this article I have sought to outline some of the perspectives brought to our 'use of the Bible in ethics' by contemporary theologians. Approaches of the sort commended above have been accused of two failings: first, that they tend towards a form of communitarian or ecclesial fundamentalism; and, second, that they fail to offer specific enough guidance in particular ethical dilemmas.

It will, I hope, be clear that neither of these objections is fair. The second is perhaps more easily dismissed, because it seems to assume that the complexities of contemporary life are susceptible to relatively simple ethical answers, transposed from the different contexts of the world of the Bible. To argue against this is not to collude in the dualism of the essay question, by divorcing the 'culturally conditioned' worlds of scripture from our own cultural conditioning. Rather, it is to argue that our world and that of the Bible are related and made one in the continuity of Christian faith and practice in the Church of the past two millennia. The ethical truths of the Bible are not given to us in lapidary, pre-packaged form. They are found in the struggle to live a Christian life; in the continual pattern of sin, repentance and renewal: 'Christian language takes it for granted … that meanings are learned and produced, not given in iconic, ahistorical form'.[18] Thus we read the Bible to shape our lives in God's image, not to seek precise answers to isolated ethical dilemmas.

The first objection, that such readings seem to favour a form of dogmatic domination by the Church, is equally misguided, if at first sight more plausible. It stems from a misunderstanding of the Church and of doctrinal orthodoxy, which sees them both as a straightjacket on the freedom of the Christian believer rather than as the guardian and enabler of that freedom. Admittedly there are many instances – in the present-day life of the Church as well as in its history – which seem to substantiate such a misreading. Yet at its best the Church has always sought to preserve an openness to the truth of God as set forth in the Scriptures and lived out in the continuing earthly Body of Christ, which is the company of believers (the *corpus christianorum* formed by the eucharist into the *corpus christi*). The continual interplay of the Bible and the Church with and in the life of God is the context in which the Christian ethical life is lived. In it cultural conditioning and timeless truth are mysteriously one, just as they are in the scandalously particular life, death and resurrection of Jesus of Nazareth, which is the life of God to us.

This is the point made, with wonted density of expression, by John Milbank:

> Somehow, because the divine *actus* is infinite, and therefore 'interminably terminated' it comprises a non-temporal dynamic or mutual 'play' between infinite 'conclusion' of expression in the Son, and an endless 're-opening' of that conclusion by the desire of the Spirit which reinspires the paternal *arche*.[19]

This loving life of the Trinity into which we are called is the beginning and the end of our ethical life, our theology and our reading of the Bible. It is thus neither wholly closed in exclusive fundamentalism nor totally open to relativistic pluralism but continually challenges us to reshape our lives in conformity to God in Christ. As Rowan Williams puts it in a different context, 'Our main question should be neither "Am I keeping the rules?" nor "Am I being sincere and non-hurtful?" but "How much am I prepared for this to signify?".'[20] Our faithfulness to God, to the Scriptures and the Church is judged by how much we are prepared for them to signify, as we seek to live out the life of Christ. In this sense the Bible is a truly open text, calling us to continue its story. Text, Church, theology and life become one: 'But there are many other things that Jesus did; if every one of them were written down, I suppose that the world could not contain the books that would be written' (John 21: 25).

Edmund Newey is rector of St Mary's, Newmarket, and St Agnes', Exning, Suffolk.

NOTES

1 Cp. R. D. Williams, *On Christian Theology* (Oxford: Blackwell, 1999), p. 44.

2 '...biblical theology's persistent concern with its own disciplinary integrity leads [it] to bracket out constructive theological convictions': S. Fowl, *Engaging Scripture: A Model for Theological Interpretation* (Oxford: Blackwell, 1998), p. 1.

3 As Tracy puts it, 'To make the text into the revelation is to turn Christianity into a strict religion of the book on the model of the place of the Qur'an in Islam': D. Tracy, *On Naming the Present: God, Hermeneutics and the Church* (London: SCM, 1994), p. 121.

4 S. Hauerwas, 'On Doctrine and Ethics', in C. Gunton (ed.), *The Cambridge Companion to Christian Ethics* (Cambridge: CUP, 1997), p. 21.

5 *Ibid.*, p. 29.

6 *Ibid.*, p. 33.

7 *Ibid.*, p. 36.

8 Fowl, *Engaging Scripture*, p. 34.

9 *Ibid.*

10 *Ibid.*, p. 55

11 R. D. Williams, *Arius: Heresy and Tradition* (London: SCM, 1987), p. 108.

12 D. Yeago, 'The New Testament and Nicene Dogma: a contribution to the recovery of theological exegesis', in S.E. Fowl, *The Theological Interpretation of Scripture: Classical and Contemporary Readings* (Oxford: Blackwell, 1997), pp. 88 and 97.

13 N. Lash, Ministry of the Word or Comedy and Philology', in *New Black-friars* (6), 1987, p. 473.

14 Fowl, *Engaging Scripture*, p. 154.

15 *Ibid.*, p. 91.

16 N. Lash *Theology on the Way to Emmaus* (London: SCM, 1986), p. 45.

17 *Ibid.*, p. 46.

18 Williams, *On Christian Theology* (1999), p. 49.

19 J. Milbank, *The Word Made Strange: Theology, Language, Culture* (Oxford: Blackwell, 1997), p. 187.

20 R. D. Williams 'Is there a Christian sexual ethic?', in *Open to Judgement* (London: DLT, 1994), p. 167.

Radical Orthodoxy: A Review

SIMON OLIVER

One afternoon in the early autumn of 1998, a group of twenty or so Cambridge theologians, including John Milbank, Catherine Pickstock, Graham Ward and a number of their research students, gathered to discuss a growing theological consensus amongst their number. At that meeting, it was decided to publish a collection of essays which would draw together under one title some of the disparate research projects of the contributors. Such significant patterns of agreement and the spontaneous desire to contribute to a common project are unusual in academic theology: here was an opportunity to make an initial attempt to speak of a vision which was slowly emerging. The volume of essays would also act as a pilot for an extensive series of theological works which would develop these initial themes and concerns in more detail. The result was the provocatively titled *Radical Orthodoxy: A New Theology* edited by John Milbank, Catherine Pickstock and Graham Ward.[1]

Four years on, the *Radical Orthodoxy* series encompasses many and various works, from John Milbank and Catherine Pickstock's *Truth in Aquinas* to Stephen Long's *Divine Economy: Theology and the Market.*[2] In this sense, the first collection of essays can be regarded as something of a success: it continues to rally many young theologians from various denominational backgrounds to write under the banner of its title. But what is the vision articulated in that first provocative and controversial volume? Does this collection offer us a coherent and appealing theology? In what sense, if at all, is this a 'new' theology? This review seeks to address these questions. Elsewhere in this edition of *Third Millennium*, others offer a more detailed view of radical orthodoxy and its aims. I begin with my own brief account of what I understand by radical orthodoxy as this is articulated in the initial collection of essays before selecting just three of the essays for special comment.

In the modern university, although we make a pretence at 'interdisciplinary study', the boundaries between different subjects and discourses are carefully policed: biology deals with living organisms, medicine deals more particularly with the human body, politics deals with social organization and institutions, history deals with the past, geography deals with space, astronomy deals with the planets and the stars, economics deals with the allocation of scarce resources, media studies deal with mass technological communication. Amidst the bewildering multiplication of disciplines in modern education, Christian theology seems to have found a very small corner to inhabit, somewhere adjacent to religious studies. This corner includes the Bible, Church history, the nature and content of Christian doctrine and theological ethics. Apparently, these are the things with which theologians are concerned, and they stray beyond their particular remit at their peril.

As John Milbank so brilliantly and provocatively argued in his *Theology and Social Theory*,[3] it was not always thus. Confining theology to one corner of intellectual, educational and social life involves opening a space from which theology – and by association all speech about God – is apparently excluded. In other words, as theology (and Christian life) is confined, a new space is opened, the space known as the 'secular'. There was a time when there was no secular, when theology was not so confined. Theology was not limited to the categories which we would now associate with a degree course in theology or preparation for ministry in the Church. Augustine, Grosseteste, Aquinas, Nicholas of Cusa and many others wrote treatises on kingship, history, political organization, optics, the physics of moving bodies, the motions of the planets and so on. They did so as theologians. Their concerns were so wide ranging because they believed that nothing could ultimately be known outside of its relation to God, the source, goal and primary cause of all things. In the end, all sciences were in some way analogically related to theology as the queen of the sciences. Take Augustine as an example, for whom 'curiosity' or 'disinterested investigation', the motivating force behind so much modern intellectual life, is decadent. One investigates creation because it is God's, it speaks of his glory and it cannot be fully known outside of its relation to its origin and goal. Such a vision lends a theological tenor to all human enquiry.

The increasing separation of different human intellectual disciplines in the period that we call 'modernity' (roughly, from about the sixteenth century, but having its origins much earlier) might be thought to be an inevitable consequence of progress in human knowledge. One might also think that the separation of intellectual disciplines makes possible specialization in, for example, natural science, which in turn makes possible the scientific revolution and progress towards 'enlightenment'. Much of the work of radical orthodoxy's immediate intellectual forebears (particularly Milbank's earlier work) attempts to show, amongst many other things, that this increasing division of the sciences, the strict delineation of the limits of theological discourse and the concomitant rise of the secular are far from innocent and do not pertain to an unambiguous 'progress'. Along with the separation of discourses comes the sense that nature and humanity can be properly known without any reference to a transcendent origin and goal.

It is well beyond the purview of this review to develop these arguments in any detail, save to say that radical orthodoxy is concerned to break beyond the boundaries within which modern academic theology and religious life have been bound. So theology is not only concerned with revelation, the doctrine of God, Biblical hermeneutics and Ecclesiastical history, but also with politics, economics, communication, social theory, biology, the nature of history, aesthetics and so on. It is not that radical orthodoxy attempts to offer weird alternatives to already established disciplines. But radical orthodoxy does attempt to offer theological accounts of categories which traditionally fall within the remit of 'secular' discourses. It does so because it unapologetically refuses to accept the ultimate sufficiency and validity of a purely secular realm of enquiry.

How is this vision articulated in the collection of articles entitled *Radical Orthodoxy*? In this book, one will not find essays dealing exclusively with 'Christology', 'The Trinity' or 'The Synoptic Problem'. Instead, one finds essays under headings such as 'Language', 'Friendship', 'Erotics', 'Bodies', 'Perception', 'Aesthetics' and 'Music'. Here, theological discourse is self-consciously creeping beyond its commonly conceived boundaries. As one progresses through this volume, one is struck by the way in which this dense, bold (some would say cavalier) writing is a clarion call to theology to turn from what John Milbank has elsewhere called its 'false humility'. This false humility accepts the boundaries traced for theology and the Church by modern intellectual and social life and operates within those limits. The contributors to this volume are offering a much more confident vision of a theology which, as in pre-modernity, is present amidst all search for truth in order to point us to God who is truth. In this sense, I think the volume of essays and the project at large is 'radical' when viewed against the priorities and limits set for theology in modernity.

Amongst the alluring titles in this collection, one in particular stands out as belonging to a more conventional understanding of the subject matter and limits of theology, namely John Montag's contribution under the heading 'Revelation'. Yet this essay is one which most clearly defies the boundaries drawn for modern theology, precisely because it argues that there is no such thing as 'revelation' understood as an identifiable sphere of distinct knowledge and information wholly independent from all others. Montag, a Jesuit now teaching at Creighton University in the US, states:

> certain trends in modern theology fail to come to terms with the origin of the notion of revelation from within modernity itself … Given that so many Christian theologians, both Catholic and Protestant, regard revelation as the most fundamental category, this lacuna takes on particular significance for any account of theology within modernity. (p. 38)

Montag argues that the identification of 'revelation' as a sphere of special information helps to delineate revelation as a particular and bounded subject matter for theology. He suggests that the identification of the boundaries of revelation is a curiously modern phenomenon, beginning around the seventeenth century and particularly with the Spanish Jesuit theologian Francisco Suárez (1548–1617). Montag notes that, around the time of Suárez, treatises abound concerning the nature and extent of revelation: this sphere of 'information' becomes the delimited subject matter of theologians. The thought of Suárez is elegantly contrasted with that of Thomas Aquinas (1225–1274), who never felt it necessary to write a treatise on revelation because he did not understand revelation to be a category of autonomous and special knowledge. For Aquinas, argues Montag,

> revelation has to do primarily with one's perspective on things in the light of one's final end [i.e. the vision of God]. It is not a supplementary packet of information about 'facts' which are around the bend, as it were, from rational comprehension or physical observation … Revelation is received as a gift; but it does not help to imagine a 'revelation' prior to the reception, as if already set aside by God before his giving it and our taking it in. (p. 43)

This is not to say that for Aquinas there is no such thing as revelation. Montag is only reminding us that, for Aquinas, revelation does not establish an autonomous realm of enquiry which is 'as it were, around the bend from rational comprehension'. So for Aquinas, revelation and rational comprehension are not separate; revelation doesn't just deliver the bits which are beyond human reason. Rather, revelation and reason intermingle, for the latter helps us to clarify and articulate the implications of the former. This refusal to accept a bounded sphere of knowledge called revelation apparently independent of reason as the subject matter of theology is indicative of the radical orthodoxy project at large. Keeping theology within the sphere of a special revelation keeps theology *out* of other disciplines and confines theology to an increasingly private sphere of special knowledge. On such a view, special knowledge only has significance for those who believe they have received that knowledge. So religion becomes an increasingly private activity confined to a subjective personal choice rather than a shared public activity. This is a gnosticism which radical orthodoxy refuses as it extends theological enquiry into spheres which, for those of us more used to the comfortably bounded world of the modern Church, may be unfamiliar.

We see the extension of theological enquiry in Graham Ward's essay under that heading 'Bodies'. Ward, Professor of Contextual Theology and Ethics at the University of Manchester and an Anglican priest, seems, like Montag, to be operating within familiar theological bounds. His essay concerns what he calls 'the displaced body of Jesus'. Ward examines the way in which the body of Jesus 'is physically human and subject to all the infirmities of being such, and yet is also a body looking backward to the perfect Adamic corporeality and forward to the corporeality of resurrection' (p. 164). Taking the gospel narratives, Ward notes that the body of Christ takes different forms and meanings as it is, as it were, gradually 'displaced' towards its final resurrection form. At the transfiguration, for example, 'the physical body of Jesus is displaced – for it is not the physical body as such which is the source of the attraction but the glorification of the physical body made possible by viewing him through God as God' (p. 166). At the Eucharist, the displacement becomes more abrupt because 'transfiguration turns into transposition'. The inauguration of the Eucharist on the night of Jesus' betrayal marks the beginning of the handing over of his body (to us for our nourishment in the Eucharist, to the Roman and Jewish authorities in Christ's surrender) and on towards crucifixion. The body of Jesus is again 'displaced' in the resurrection and the ascension. Ward states that 'the ascension is the final displacement of the body of the gendered Jew. The final displacement rehearses the logic of the eucharist: the body itself is transposed. A verse from Colossians elucidates this: "The Church is his body, the fullness of him who fills all in all."' (pp. 175–6).

Amidst the analysis of the displacement of Christ's body, Ward continually points to the displacement away from a gendered male body with the attendant desires and erotics, towards the Church made by the Eucharist as the ungendered body of Christ and a differently orientated ecclesial community of erotic desire – the community of love which is continually drawn to Christ. There are implications for our notions of love and the Church, and the meaning, role and nature of the body. Space prohibits further elucidation of these themes. However, this contribution does demonstrate some aspects of the project of radical orthodoxy. The essay takes as its subject matter categories which are usually confined to discourses other than theology: the body (which is usually confined to biology or social theory), erotics and desire (usually confined to psychology), and the masculine and feminine (now usually confined to gender or political studies). Ward reads and understands these categories in and through the Christian narrative of Jesus Christ and places them within the ambit of more familiar theological themes: incarnation, transfiguration, resurrection, the Eucharist, the Church and so on. On the way, Ward refers to numerous works, from Jacques Lacan's *Four Fundamental Concepts of Psycho-Analysis* to Gregory of Nyssa's thirteenth sermon on the *Song of Songs*. Yet this remains a resolutely theological reading of the body and desire, one which does not surrender legitimacy to purely secular readings of these categories.

Catherine Pickstock, now a lecturer in the philosophy of religion at Cambridge, shows in a different way the extension of theological enquiry into territory not wholly familiar to the modern theologian. She analyses the metaphysical category of music with particular reference to Augustine's treatise *De Musica*. Many of us would assume that music is not metaphysical at all, but an aesthetic category more allied to sound and entertainment. Yet the pre-modern tradition would not see concepts and categories as separated in this way. In so far as music could be an aesthetic category, it would have a metaphysical basis and, ultimately, a theological ground. So, for example, the category of music for Pythagoras and, following him, Plato, concerns proportion and mathematics, beauty and order. The Pythagoreans knew that harmonious sounds and the pitches of notes could be expressed by number. Moreover, they did not think that such expression was accidental or incidental to the way things are. The same proportions and harmonies one finds in music-making are also found in nature between, for example, the harmonious proportions of the plants and the stars. So in his cosmological treatise *Timaeus*, Plato, following many of his predecessors, talks of 'the music of the heavenly spheres'. By this, he means the mathematically describable harmonies and proportions which constitute the universe. Yet this is not mere metaphor: there is a genuine analogy between the harmonies involved in music making and the harmonies of the cosmos. Moreover, that analogy is the reason why we find both to be beautiful. So aesthetics – the notion of beauty – is not at all to do with subjective taste but is written into the fabric of creation. We recognize this harmonious beauty because we are ourselves part of the harmonious beauty of creation: there is a kinship (including a common origin and goal) between us and nature. Music expresses that kinship.

So Pickstock is concerned with 'the *musica mundana*' which 'overlapped in its concerns with astronomy, as the heavenly spheres were thought to compose through their movements and ratios a music unhearable by us'. Music had two further classifications, namely:

> the *musica humana*, which concerned the harmonies between the body and soul as well as the musical relationships within both the body and soul, and the *musica instumentalis*, which concerned aspects of audible music governed either by tension upon a string, by breath, by water, or by percussion. (p.243)

Pickstock traces music's connection not only with cosmology but also with ethics, politics and law. Once again, this reveals the project of radical orthodoxy as one which seeks to destabilize modernity's arbitrary sectioning of the areas of human life and intellectual enquiry.

Pickstock's central argument concerns the reality of aesthetics and perception to which I have already alluded: the beautiful is not a matter of the merely subjective appreciation of phenomena. The beautiful – the harmonious music of the cosmos – is real and ultimately founded on the participation of the cosmos in the beauty and perfect harmony of the Trinitarian life of God. Pickstock subverts an important modern dualism which many works in the radical orthodoxy series contest, namely that between subject and object. We are not subjects perceiving objects in the universe – this would be to understand ourselves as in some way 'outside' or fundamentally different to the universe. Rather, the whole is composed of *creatures of God*, and our kinship understood as a shared creaturely nature is the basis for our knowing the cosmos and our sharing with all creation in the music of divine praise.

I have described just three of the twelve essays which compose the volume. There is a common concern to extend the limits of theological enquiry and to understand categories theologically. Do the remaining essays lie within this trajectory so as to form a coherent project? There is certainly a common desire to return to the pre-modern tradition when theology and Christian life was not so confined within secular bounds. Yet this is not nostalgia, for the ancient sources concerning, for example, the city or aesthetics, are applied within our current postmodern context in which we flounder to articulate a shared tradition, rationality and ethics. Radical orthodoxy sees this 'postmodern condition' as the logical outworking of modernity, and at the same time as an opportunity to break the shackles by which modernity has bound theology and the Christian life.

However, this collection is the spontaneous drawing together of many and various research projects, some of which were still at an early stage of development. It does not have the coherent character of a set of specifically commissioned or selected works. For that reason, *Radical Orthodoxy* does appear very much as the initial attempt to articulate a shared vision. The writing is frequently dense and occasionally convoluted. Prospective readers should expect to encounter the unfamiliar names of continental philosophers and social theorists – Irigaray, Deleuze, Lacan – many of which are not encountered in Anglo-American universities and theological colleges. Some of the essays will appeal more to the academic specialist, particularly John Milbank's characteristically superb essay on the German eighteenth-century radical pietists Johann Georg Hamann and Franz Heinrich Jacobi. Milbank is particularly concerned to avoid the charge that radical orthodoxy writes off modernity wholesale without subtlety in order to return nostalgically to the pre-modern. In the work of Hamann and Jacobi he finds an orthodox, rather than modern, theology at work.

I gave this collection to a friend shortly after its publication and he commented that it was like intruding on a private conversation. In a sense, one can sympathize with that view. On the one hand, references abound to philosophers and social theorists who will be largely unfamiliar to the British or American reader trained purely in modern theology and biblical criticism. Also, in order to understand the thrust of *Radical Orthodoxy*, one has first to appreciate the opportunity it sees at the present time for theology and the Church. The excellent introduction to the volume will help in this regard. Also, one might read *Radical Orthodoxy* alongside a collection of articles entitled *Radical Orthodoxy – A Catholic Enquiry?* edited by Laurence Paul Hemming.[4] This collection includes some reactions to the first volume and some very clear explanations of the nature of the radical orthodoxy project, particularly from John Milbank.

So is *Radical Orthodoxy: A new theology* genuinely new and what does it offer? Of course, there is an important sense in which the contributors would regard this work of theology as not at all new, namely in its desire faithfully to recover a pre-modern, traditional mode of theological enquiry. Also, the contributors would not claim their theology as their own. Their work seeks to articulate the theology of the Church, and this is surely not 'new' in the way in which a trend or fad might be 'new'. Moreover, as the acknowledgements state, the contributors to this volume, including the editors, are themselves deeply indebted to a number of their teachers whose writings began to set the agenda of radical orthodoxy (Nicholas Lash, Emeritus Professor of Theology at Cambridge, Archbishop Rowan Williams and the American Christian ethicist Stanley Hauerwas are three obvious examples). But this collection does herald a new confidence in theological writing. In these pages one finds an assuredness in speaking to the world about some of its most basic categories, but in a fashion that is not governed by non-theological methods and norms. As I have attempted to suggest in this review, the contributors are breaking beyond the commonly conceived boundaries of theology, and hence they begin to question the boundaries established by other disciplines. This only serves to point to the enormous intellectual demands of such a project. The tendency to deploy the thought of so many thinkers from so many eras and traditions can lead to a haphazard and confused conflagration which does not issue in clarity. This collection does occasionally suffer under the weight of its own ambition. For example, one should place Lacan's psychoanalysis alongside Gregory of Nyssa's sermon on the *Song of Songs* with great care and sensitivity (as I believe Graham Ward does). Yet this only serves to demonstrate the weighty challenge of doing theology in the context of a diverse and disordered postmodernity.

So *Radical Orthodoxy* reminds us of the difficulty of doing theology and the need to read the world in terms of the traditional theological categories of Church, Eucharist, Trinity, Incarnation and so on, rather than reading these theological categories in terms of secular methods and norms. The hardpressed parish priest might wonder why she should bother with this dense and difficult writing. In these pages, one finds the very demanding call to extend the limits of theology, and likewise the limits of the Christian life and the Church, beyond the bounds of subjective, private choice. We all need a good dose of this new radically orthodox confidence.

Simon Oliver is chaplain of Hertford College, Oxford.

NOTES

1　John Milbank, Catherine Pickstock and Graham Ward (eds), *Radical Orthdoxy: A New Theology* (London: Routledge, 1999).

2　Catherine Pickstock, *Truth in Aquinas* (London: Routledge, 2001); Stephen Long, *Divine Economy: Theology and the Market* (London: Routledge, 2000).

3　John Milbank, *Theology and Social Theory* (Oxford: Blackwell, 1990).

4　Laurence Paul Hemming (ed.), *Radical Orthodoxy – A Catholic Enquiry?* (Aldershot: Ashgate, 2000).

Theological Integrity: A Brief Introduction to the Thought of Rowan Williams

EDMUND NEWEY

Christian theology takes as its subject matter *all things in relation to God*. This was the refrain taught to generations of Cambridge undergraduates by Professor Nicholas Lash, perhaps the most prominent of Rowan Williams' theological mentors. Lash's influence, with that of his predecessor Donald MacKinnon, is apparent in almost all of Williams' published work. Like them both, Williams shows by the range of his concerns a firm belief in the duty of theology to concern itself with *all things*, whilst resisting the triumphalist claim that as 'queen of the sciences' it can place all other discourses at its beck and call. And yet, generous though he is in acknowledging his indebtedness to these and other teachers, Williams has gone beyond them in range and depth. So far he has not attempted a systematic theology, but his writing, especially in view of his pastoral commitments, is almost unparalleled in its scope, rigour and theological integrity. One anonymous bishop observed in the *Church Times* that, with Rowan Williams as Archbishop of Canterbury, the Church of England would be blessed with 'a new Anselm', and it is certainly true that one has to go a long way back in history to discover a Primate held in such esteem by the foremost theologians of the day.

This enthusiastic reception has not been without dissenting voices. Some Evangelicals have objected that his moral views show him to be a man who fails 'to take the Bible seriously', whilst a number of the less thoughtful conservatives of all churchmanships have been misled by the journalistic tag 'liberal' into questioning his doctrinal orthodoxy. These criticisms have, however, mainly come from those who have engaged with his thought only superficially. A more plausible objection has been that his work is too abstruse for the majority of his potential audience. Some of his writings are, undoubtedly, demanding even to trained theologians, and he takes a certain delight in contributing to recondite journals and *Festchriften* for little-known continental theologians. Yet his more popular works – the Lent books, *The Truce of God* and *Christ on Trial*, the meditations on the Virgin Mary in *Ponder These Things*, the sermons collected in *Open to Judgement* and his newspaper articles (some of which are available in *Darkness Yielding*) – reveal an ability to communicate in a far more accessible idiom.[1] In fact, in one week in late 2002, five of the *Church Times*' top ten religious books were by Rowan Williams.

Theologians, like academics in general, tend to divide into two categories: those who write too little and those who write too much. The German-speaking giants of the last century, Barth, Rahner and Balthasar, wrote at a length beyond the capacity of most readers, whilst English-speaking theologians, with the odd prolific exception such as John Macquarrie, tend to err on the side of excessive reticence. In a way Rowan Williams falls into both camps. He has written too much that is scattered in scholarly journals found only in university libraries, and too little that is easily available. In fact, until the publication of the essays collected in *On Christian Theology*,[2] the range of his work was barely known outside the scholarly community. In addition to his ten or so books, the bibliography of major essays extends to well over one hundred items. His subjects include art and literature, politics both domestic and international, philosophy, church history, feminism, sexuality and – within the field of theology – Eastern Orthodoxy, patristics, monasticism, pastoral, philosophical, sacramental and Liberation theology, and the theological interpretation of scripture. He has also published translations from French, German and Russian and two volumes of theologically-significant poetry.

In the brief space available here I shall take 'soundings' into a number of the subject areas mentioned above, referring principally to his less widely known writings, before making some more general observations in conclusion.

Politics

Rowan Williams' self-description as a 'hairy leftie' is well known, as is his involvement with direct-action CND campaigning in the early 1980s. His commitment to a broadly socialist and pacifist outlook is nonetheless far from uncritical. In a juxtaposition of the mediaeval with the modern that is one of the hallmarks of his thought, he observes in a recent essay that Thomas Aquinas's trinitarian theology has implications that can help us to see 'that Marx's apocalyptic gulf between those who seek to *understand* and those who seek to *change* the world is already bridged in Thomas'.[3] In saying this, Williams does not deny the Marxist insight that politics belongs in the realm of history rather than that of 'the natural'. He does, however, insist on the vital part played by the Church as a sacramental community witnessing to the fact that 'it is God and not any existing social form which fundamentally defines human existence'. The Church's vocation, then, is to 'summon all of us to a theological critique of our social context, and to a more historically concrete understanding of the pressures of the coming Kingdom'.[4]

This liberationist understanding of the task of theology is also evident in his 1982 book *Resurrection*, where he critiques and extends the political theology of the German Catholic Johann Baptist Metz. To Metz's demand that the Church must challenge the world with the 'memory of suffering', of which she is the subversive guardian, he adds the nuance that this challenge is also an invitation, embodied in the sacramental reality of 'the Church's human and relational life'.[5]

This perspective finds its most complete expression in a demanding essay, which is the fruit of his friendship with the Jewish philosopher Gillian Rose. Inspired by Rose's conception of 'the broken middle' – the disputed but fruitful ground between opposing systematic certainties – as the site for political action, Williams strives to express the way in which the Church must resist premature security and imitate the vocation of Israel, the people of God, whose identity is inextricably bound up with exile. In this light the cross of Christ and the image of the Church as a 'resident alien' both suggest the same paradoxical vocation to realize 'a corporate life whose critical practice constantly challenges sectional interest and proprietorial models of power or knowledge'.[6] Here in the human narrative of God's ever-greater initiative, constantly renewed in this broken middle ground 'between politics and metaphysics', we find the basis for the Church's imitation of and sharing in the divinely human life of Christ.

Philosophy

Williams also owes to Gillian Rose perhaps the most prominent U-turn of his intellectual biography, his reassessment of the philosophy of Hegel. Over the last two hundred years the relevance of Hegel's philosophy to theology has been much debated. Initially Williams broadly subscribed to the widespread view that Hegel's philosophical system, despite its evident intention to take history seriously, finishes by evading the realm of time. In his 1989 essay, 'Trinity and Ontology' (republished in *On Christian Theology*) he criticizes Hegel's excessively abstract understanding of the life of the Trinity and his tendency to generalize 'Good Friday into a necessary moment in the historical dialectic'.[7] From Rose, however, Williams learned an alternative perspective, which sees in Hegel both a creative restatement of Christian faith and a challenge to what she regarded as the premature desire in much postmodern thought for an apolitical transcendence of mundane reality. Helpful as Jacques Derrida's deconstructionist project may be in warning of the dangers of the 'glib historicism' into which Hegel sometimes falls, Williams asks whether 'the Derridean construal of the arbitrariness of communication ... remove[s] from language its critical and liberative possibilities'? Against this danger, Williams follows Rose in seeking to renew the Hegelian project to defend a religious tradition that affirms both the 'divine liberty and [the] divine "commitment" to a historical life and a social practice, whose mark of godliness is self-critical vigilance (what used to be called repentance, I think)'.[8]

Patristics

Aside from his major work on Arius, Williams' most significant contribution to patristic scholarship has been his reassessment of the thought of Augustine.[9] The weight of twentieth-century thinking on Augustine's philosophy has read him as Descartes *avant la lettre*. Charles Taylor, in his excellent and influential *Sources of the Self*, concisely expresses the widely-held view that Augustine was the instigator of modernity's turn inwards, a turn that identified the essence of humanity in the reasoning of the isolated mind.[10] Whilst recognizing the pervasive nature of 'the fundamental illusion of modernity, the notion that the private self is the arbiter and source of value in the world', Williams, in common with a number of other contemporary theologians, demonstrates that this notion is actually inimical to Augustine's vision.[11] In a pair of essays which subject Augustine's *De Trinitate* to an extended critical reading, Williams points out that, in contrast to Descartes, Augustine's conception of the human self presupposes an origin in the prior and constant self-giving of God. This basis in the renewing reality of the divine gift establishes the Augustinian self as relational through and through. It is thus utterly distinct from the Cartesian self, which famously discovers its existence through a process of radical and solipsistic doubt. As Williams puts it, for Augustine, 'if we exist because God desires to impart his life, we exist as sharers in knowledge and love, as beings whose self-awareness and self-relatedness is possible in virtue of relatedness to [the] limitless knowledge and love [of God]'.[12]

Space does not allow me to examine Williams' other significant contributions to our understanding of the theology of the early Church, though it is worth noting that his essays are seldom purely historical. Characteristically they close by drawing analogies with contemporary situations, as in the long 'Theological Postscript' to *Arius* with its recognition of the critical importance of the Nicene heritage in our proclamation of the gospel today.

Systematic theology

Aside from the essays now available in *On Christian Theology*, perhaps the most stimulating of Williams' areas of research in general systematics has been his engagement with the movement known as theological non-realism. In 1984, in the first issue of the influential periodical, *Modern Theology*, he held a graceful and productive debate with the leading British non-realist, Don Cupitt. Here he accepts that he has learned much from Cupitt and that they have in common their agreement that 'the question of God [is] something which cannot be settled by supposedly neutral observation' and that language about God is not 'readily intelligible if treated as [the] description of an individual or object'. The essence of his disagreement with Cupitt, however, lies in his concern about the danger non-realism runs of domesticating the otherness of God: 'religious practice claims to offer liberation: but if God is conceived as yet another bundle of stimuli for the greedy self, and if our relation with God takes on the "interesting" character of a personal love affair ... how on earth can it liberate'?[13]

As Williams admits in his introduction to Colin Crowder's 1997 volume *God and Reality*, there is in a bishop's treatment of non-realism always the possibility that 'hierarchical nervousness' may cloud the vision, but he is clear in his recognition that the debate is not about *whether* God exists so much as about *how* that existence is to be portrayed.[14] His preference remains firmly for the realist picture, principally because it alone seems sufficiently open to the 'significant element of the passive or receptive' in our attempts to speak of God. Prayer and praise – both engaging with something really other – help us to 'begin the purgation of fantasy in our moral life by grasping that consciousness is not self-created and [that] therefore [the] will cannot be a straightforward absolute'.[15]

Anglicanism

The depth of Rowan Williams' knowledge and love of the Anglican tradition has recently been demonstrated by his contribution to the anthology, *Love's Redeeming Work*.[16] He edited and introduced the first section, covering the period from 1530 to 1650. The selection of texts covers a range extending well beyond the familiar territory of the great sixteenth-century English Reformers and the Caroline divines of the seventeenth century. One of the most interesting inclusions is that of a number of excerpts from Shakespeare. As Williams admits in the introduction, Shakespeare is 'not likely to have been a very reliable member of the Reformed Church of England', but his plays do contain 'striking echoes, parodies and enlargements of biblical and theological language', which are an indispensable part of his whole imaginative outlook.[17]

The central place in Williams' appreciation of Anglicanism is taken, however, by Richard Hooker. His essay, 'Richard Hooker: Philosopher, Anglican, Contemporary', has been influential in the scholarly community but remains hard to obtain. Recent commentary on Hooker has tended to emphasize the origin of the *Laws of Ecclesiastical Polity* in controversial debate with the Puritans and has thus questioned its semi-canonical status in Anglican tradition. Williams does not dispute the *Laws*' polemical origins, but, drawing on its continuity with the thought of Thomas Aquinas, he shows how Hooker goes back behind many of the developments of late mediaeval and early Reformation theology to draw on the Thomist synthesis of the Augustinian and Aristotelian traditions. This is apparent above all in Hooker's attitude to the debates about 'voluntarism', the movement of thought within late mediaeval scholasticism, which emphasized the absolute power of God (and the arbitrary ways in which such power was held to take concrete form in the universe). Hooker questions the 'voluntarist' tendency to conceive of God as an abstractly opposed Other and insists that the participation of humanity in the mystery God is the ground of our being. At heart his theology is based on the pursuit of wisdom, a pursuit entailing

> both a positive and a modest valuation of the human: positive in that we alone in all creation have as our goal the enjoyment of 'beauty in it self' ... ; modest in that there is an unbridgeable gap between our finite capacity and the object that satisfies it'[18]

Here in Hooker we find one of the sources for a central theme of Williams' own theology, the emphasis on our growth into God in and over time, through the slow and never-completed process of learning and 'learning about learning' that characterizes the Christian life.

Conclusion

As Williams observes, Hooker's legacy is one that has much to offer in the contemporary scene, where 'the theological debate so readily polarizes between one or another variety of positivism (biblically fundamentalist, ecclesiastically authoritarian, or whatever) and a liberalism without critical or self-critical edge'.[19] Much of the intolerance and impatience of modern life, as he argues in *Lost Icons*, stems from the reluctance to open our lives to the questioning of God, 'the Other who does not compete ... who will not be evaded or deflected, yet has and seeks no advantage'.[20]

I have attempted to give an introduction to some of the recurrent themes of Rowan Williams' theological reflection. To summarize so wide-ranging a body of work is impossible, but certain underlying themes do emerge. First, in contradistinction to the characteristically postmodern 'hermeneutic of suspicion', Williams's mode of enquiry is what might be called a hermeneutic of 'trustful interrogation'. This is a phrase he uses in the essay 'Trinity and Revelation', an essay which lies at the heart of his theological method and forms the central chapter of *On Christian Theology*. In context the phrase refers to our approach as believers to the foundational events of faith in the life of Jesus Christ, but it captures something about the whole spirit of Williams' thought: critical but not destructive, trusting but not naïve. Second, he shows a repeated interest in the territory identified by Gillian Rose as the 'broken middle'. I would not wish to assimilate this too easily to the Anglican *via media*, with its unhelpful associations of effortless superiority and the complacency of establishment. Yet there is a sense in which Williams' whole theology is a renewal of the Anglican middle way, very much on the lines called for in Peter Walker's important but overlooked book of the late 1980s.[21] Third, there is a constant concern for theological integrity. Such integrity does not derive from a spurious claim to a total perspective (which, if it were made, would be tantamount to a blasphemous claim to divinity). Instead, it is a desire to seek a unity that does not impose uniformity but is prepared patiently 'to make connections, to search out and display unities or analogies'.[22]

Finally and perhaps most importantly of all, Williams' theology combines a deep love of Christian doctrine with a recognition of its limits. He believes that:

> [The] great and lasting revivals of Christian spiritual seriousness (the monastic revival of the twelfth century, the Reformation, the new religious movements associated with Teresa of Avila or Ignatius Loyola, the Methodist revival in England and Wales, the early days of the ecumenical movement in [the twentieth] century) have all been occasions for the renewal of doctrinal depth and passion for the rediscovery of the dense and vital texture of creedal truth.[23]

Yet he also understands the reticence necessary before the mystery of God. In its positive concern with all things, theology must also recognize its negative duty to purify our words about God, discerning the point when it 'has said what it can say and when it is time to shut up'.[24]

NOTES

1 *The Truce of God* (London: Fount Paperbacks, 1983); *Christ on Trial* (London: Fount, 2000); *Ponder These Things* (Norwich: Canterbury Press, 2002); *Open to Judgement* (London: DLT, 1994); *Darkness Yielding* (Sheffield: Cairns Publications, 2001).

2 *On Christian Theology* (Oxford: Blackwell, 2000).

3 'What does love Know? Saint Thomas on the Trinity, *New Blackfriars* (82), 2001, p. 272.

4 *Politics and Theological Identity* (London: Jubilee Group 1984) [with David Nicholls], p. 17, p. 24.

5 *Resurrection: Interpreting the Easter Gospel* (London: DLT, 1982), p. 67.

6 'Between Politics and Metaphysics: Reflections in the Wake of Gillian Rose', *Modern Theology*, 1995, p. 19.

7 *On Christian Theology*, p. 161.

8 'Hegel and the gods of postmodernity', in Berry, Wernick (eds) *Shadow of Spirit: Postmodernism and Religion*, (London, 1992), p. 79.

9 *Arius: Heresy and Tradition* (London: DLT, 1986).

10 *Sources of the Self* (Cambridge: CUP, 1989).

11 'Sapientia and the Trinity; Reflections on the *De Trinitate*' in Bruning (ed.) *Collectanea Augustiniana, Melanges T.J. van Bavel* (Leuven:

Leuven UP, 1990), p. 317. See also 'The Paradoxes of Self-knowledge in the *De Trinitate*' in Liebhard (ed.) *Collectanea Augustiniana* (New York: Peter Lang, 1993).

12 'Sapientia', p. 321.

13 'Religious Realism: On Not Quite Agreeing with Don Cupitt', *Modern Theology* (1), 1984, p. 4.

14 *God and Reality* (London: Mowbray, 1997).

15 'Religious Realism', p.9.

16 *Love's Redeeming Work* (Oxford: OUP, 2001).

17 *Ibid.*, p. 8.

18 'Richard Hooker: Philosopher, Anglican, Contemporary', in A. S. McGrade (ed.), *Richard Hooker and the Construction of Christian Community* (Tempe, AZ: 1997), p. 372.

19 'Richard Hooker', p. 383

20 *Lost Icons: Reflections on Cultural Bereavement* (Edinburgh: T&T Clark, 2000), p. 186.

21 Peter Walker, *Rediscovering the Middle Way* (London: Mowbray, 1988).

22 *On Christian Theology*, p. 14.

23 ''The Seal of Orthodoxy': Mary and the Heart of Christian Doctrine', in Martin Warner (ed.), *Say Yes to God* (London: Tufton Books, 1999), p. 16.

24 *On Christian Theology*, p. 15.

A Sermon in Season

SIMON OLIVER

Isaiah 40.18–31
Acts 16.16–34

Have you met any particularly powerful people? A powerful public speaker, maybe, or a politician? I'm going to talk about power – not about powerful people but about the power of God – and I'd like to do that by taking you through the passage from the book of the Acts of the Apostles which forms the second reading. Now this book of Acts was written by St Luke, the same Luke who wrote one of the four gospels which tell us about the life of Jesus. The book of Acts is the account of the very first years of the Church and the growth of Christianity, about the life of the followers of Jesus immediately after the resurrection. It is particularly about the conversion of a persecutor of the Christians named Saul, the man who became St Paul, and we learn a great deal about Paul's missionary journeys in the first years of Christianity. What we are going to see in the passage is the gentle nature of God's power, and how that power shows itself in uniting people. So let's look at the story.

Let me start by putting this passage in context. In this passage, narrated by Luke, St Paul and some other apostles are in Philippi, a Roman colony in what is now northern Greece. Paul had been preaching on the Sabbath outside the city walls, and we are told that many women attended Paul's sermon. One of those women, named Lydia, had come to faith and she and her household had been baptised. Now Paul's preaching seems to have attracted the attention of a strange slave-girl, and this is where we pick up the story in our reading this evening. This slave-girl had a spirit of divination – a spirit which gave her a particular sense of the divine and mystical, possibly the power to see the future – and she was owned by some people who made a great deal of money from her. The girl was forced to use her intuitive grasp of the deeply mystical and spiritual nature of life for commercial gain, and of course the irony is that because she used this spiritual intuition to make money, it is actually worthless to her. But she starts following Paul around, no doubt disrupting his sermons with heckling when she declares that Paul and the Apostles do indeed come from the Most High God and they preach a way of salvation. But notice that nobody is converted to the new Christian faith. Despite the fact that this slave-girl with special powers declares that Paul and his companions are genuine, we are not told of anyone coming to faith in Christ. Finally Paul loses his temper and screams at the spirit possessing the slave-girl: 'I order you in the name of Jesus Christ to come out of her.' The spirit leaves the girl. But now she has lost her powers, and her owners are none too pleased because they've lost an important source of income. So the slave-girl's Roman owners have Paul and his companion Silas tried, flogged and thrown in prison.

Now Paul and Silas sit in the deepest darkness of the prison in Philippi with their feet in stocks. They begin to sing, praising God even while captive. Suddenly, there is an earthquake, the doors of the prison are opened and the chains of the prisoners are unfastened. Now when Paul and Silas's jailer saw this he would have been terrified, because the Romans would blame him for the escape of the prisoners and sentence him to a par-ticularly terrible death – possibly crucifixion. So the guard loses all hope and is about to commit suicide. The earthquake and the freeing of the prisoners, an apparently spectacular show of power, don't convert the jailer to faith – on the contrary, he is urged towards his own death. He is going to take his life. Now at this point Paul and Silas could say triumphantly – 'Ha, see, our God's more powerful than you! He's opened the gates of the prison, loosened our chains and sent us to freedom!' But Paul and Silas do not do this. They stay in the prison with their jailer. It is *this* action – Paul and Silas staying with the jailer – it is this action which brings the jailer to ask his question: 'What must I do to be saved?' The jailer took Paul and Silas to his home, washed their wounds – remember, they had been beaten severely and would have been in terrible pain – and the jailer and his household were baptised without delay.

It's important that we see the details so that we can see where the power of God is revealed. The two spectacular events of this passage – the casting out of the spirit from the slave-girl and the earthquake which opened the gates of the prison – neither of these events of great power in themselves lead to anyone becoming a Christian. What was the event that led to conversion? When Paul and Silas are freed from their chains, they stand in a position of what we think is great power. They can run for it and tell the story to all the citizens of Philippi that they were freed from the depths of the prison by the awesome power of God. The trial of these men before the magistrates of the city would have been well known, and seeing these men freed from prison by God would surely bring mass conversions and success for Paul and Silas. But they don't do this. They stay behind with the one, terrified jailer, the man who is so afraid that he moves to kill himself with his sword. And the power of God is revealed when Paul and Silas stay with the jailer, standing alongside him, taking his hand very gently and leading him from suicide by his sword to the hope of the waters of baptism. That's where the power of God is most truly revealed – the power to stay alongside the terrified and the vulnerable, the jailer who thought he was so strong and powerful, but who in the face of Almighty God is nothing. And yet he is not nothing, for he is loved in Jesus Christ and reborn into the life of God.

You who are sat here this evening are gifted, talented, good people. Over your lifetime, the odds are that you will take on positions of great power and influence. I don't mean that you'll all become politicians or media moguls. But what ever profession you go in to, people will listen to you and you will have influence. If you're going to be a doctor, you'll have great power over people's lives and their health; if you're a solicitor or barrister you'll often have great power in sorting out the legal messes people get themselves into. If you become a teacher of any kind, you'll possess enormous power over the minds of your students. If you're a musician, you'll have power to influence the artistic development and cultural expression of many, many people. The list goes on. For those of you now preparing to leave this place, be mindful of the power you will possess as you get older. And remember that the greatest power you will have will be an ability to stand by and help the less powerless, the student who struggles, the annoying elderly patient who keeps coming to your surgery just because he's lonely, the family which is undergoing a devastating breakdown. Please be mindful of how you use your power.

We see in God, the all-powerful, a gentle power. The Christian claim is that in the life of Jesus of Nazareth we find a narrative which speaks about the exercise of a divine power which is not violent but peaceful, doesn't in the end opt for spectacle, but talks only and always of love. In the cross, in an apparently powerless person crucified, we find the greatest revealing of the power of God, the power to go on loving despite the violence and hatred. And that will be the greatest expression of the power you have, to go on speaking words of peace and love and standing alongside the boring, weak and vulnerable people who will cross your path day in and day out.

I leave you with some words from this evening's first lesson from the prophet Isaiah:

> God giveth power to the faint; and to them that have no might he increaseth strength. Even the youths shall faint and be weary, and the young men shall utterly fall: But they that wait upon the Lord shall renew their strength; they shall mount up with wings as eagles; they shall run, and not be weary; and they shall walk, and not faint.

To those of you who leave this place in the days ahead, may God grant you power and peace. Amen.

Book Reviews

Stanley Hauerwas · *With the Grain of the Universe* (London: SCM Press, 2001) 249 pp. Price, £13.95

Stanley Hauerwas describes himself as a 'part philosopher, part political theorist, part theologian, part ethicist'. He is known for his breadth of interests and as a sparky and engaging, if sometimes polemical, essayist in the field of Christian ethics, and this volume represents a more sustained exploration of his theology.

The book comprises Hauerwas' Gifford Lectures, given in the University of St Andrew's in 2000–2001. There is some irony here. Lord Gifford provided for a series of lectures about 'natural theology' – in other words, the lectures were to treat their subject as a strictly natural science, without any reference to or reliance upon 'any supposed special exceptional or so-called miraculous revelation'. Hauerwas asserts that Gifford's understanding of natural theology is anything but natural. Following Alasdair MacIntyre, Hauerwas questions the legitimacy of such a non-traditioned account of rationality. He laments the false humility of theology in the face of modernity. Such strictures and limitations fail to do justice to the complexity and richness of Christian theology. Where they are employed – for instance, in the work of William James and Reinhold Niebuhr – they prove to be reductionist: in the case of James, natural theology becomes little more than the psychology of religion.

By contrast, Hauerwas presents the radical 'witness' of Karl Barth, John Howard Yoder, John Paul II and Dorothy Day. Barth's radicalism lies in the fact that he begins not with human reason or religious experience or scientific discovery but by asserting that God is the subject of theology. The witness of Yoder, as a

Mennonite theologian, lies in his insight that the gospel cannot be at home in the world because it speaks of the God found in the life, death and resurrection of Christ. The death of Christ reflects the Christian vision of peace and non-violence. For Hauerwas, Yoder's importance lies in the fact that his thought demonstrates that 'the doctrine of God and non-violence are constitutive of one another'. There can be no sanctimonious piety into which the Christian can withdraw to avoid facing the harsh realities of living in the world. Lives that bear the cross reveal 'the grain of the Universe' (a phrase of Yoder's). Like Yoder, Hauerwas seeks to challenge the Constantinian accommodation of the Church to the world. The importance of John Paul II lies in his refusal to be seduced by Constantinian ambitions, his challenge to the 'culture of death' which characterizes the world and his rejection of violence. Hauerwas' central thesis is that Christianity is to be tested and vindicated in the way 'Christians must and should live' (p. 39). The truth of theological claims is inseparable from lives well lived. The life of Dorothy Day bears witness to the rejection of violence, the promotion of peace and acts of mercy. 'Because Dorothy Day existed, we can know that the church to which John Paul II and John Howard Yoder witness is not some ideal but an undeniable reality. Moreover, such a church must exist if indeed the cross and not the sword reveals to us the very grain of the universe' (p. 230).

This is a rich and rewarding volume, but Hauerwas' argument begs a complex range of epistemological questions, particularly about the character of 'witness'. Moreover, while one cannot fail to be impressed by the present Pope's extraordinary witness in his challenge to the culture of death and his rejection of violence, there are still legitimate questions to be asked about the Vatican's 'witness' in its handling of dissent, its refusal to countenance eucharistic hospitality, and its treatment of women. Do these things reflect the very grain of the universe?

Hauerwas has high expectations of those who profess to be Christians, and this volume will delight those who want to engage with some real theology. This is not one of those turgid volumes of 'prolegomena' to theology. This is the real thing, and it provides a much-needed corrective to the 'false humility' of theology. Nevertheless, one cannot help thinking that Hauerwas' contention that he is 'not even a proper theologian' suggests a certain false humility, which perhaps is not worthy of such an able exponent of Christian virtue!

Will Lamb

Tom Wright · *The Resurrection of the Son of God* (London: SPCK, 2003), 817 pp. Price, £30.00

T*he Resurrection of the Son of God* is the third volume in N.T. Wright's series on 'Christian Origins and the Question of God'. It represents an extraordinary achievement in terms of its synthesis of biblical scholarship and historical research. With over 800 pages, it's even longer than the latest Harry Potter!

In contrast to the popular myth about one of his illustrious predecessors as Bishop of Durham, Tom Wright believes that 'it really happened'. The tomb was empty. A large part of the volume is devoted to providing evidence and support for this central claim. In terms of method, Wright follows the well worn paths of the 'History of Religions School'. This approach to New Testament study emerged in Göttingen among a group of young German biblical scholars, including Hermann Gunkel and Wilhelm Bousset, at the turn of the twentieth century. For advocates of this school, 'Judaism' and 'Hellenism' provided 'the real matrix of the gospel' (a phrase of Gunkel's). They insisted on applying the most rigorous historical critical methods to early Christianity, and in particular they insisted on taking full account of its religious matrix. This stimulated the formation of critical tools such as Source criticism, but more particularly Form criticism, with its attention to the *Sitz im Leben* (situation in life) of the first Christian communities. Initially, this led to an interest in its relationship with first-century Judaism(s), but as time continued, scholars began to look for parallels between early Christianity, on the one hand, and the mystery religions and Gnosticism on the other. The label came to be associated with hypotheses about Hellenistic influences, and contrasts between Jewish and Hellenistic expressions of Christianity. It was motivated by a concern to explain some of the perceived 'novelties' in terms of Christian practice and belief during this period and it fed speculation that early Christianity lay at the interface between Judaism and Hellenism. Gunkel and Bousset have given New Testament and Patristic scholarship a significant legacy. The distinction made between Judaism and Hellenism has proved extremely influential in subsequent debate.

The first section of the book follows in this traditional vein, although the terminology is slightly modified. Wright presents a detailed survey of attitudes towards life after death in 'pagan' and 'Jewish' thought. He sees a number of significant contrasts between the two: unlike the speculation about death and Hades among Platonists and others in the pagan milieu, Jewish beliefs in the resurrection presented an account, not so much of life after death, but *life after* life after death. In other words, there would be an intermediate state between death and the resurrection at some point in the future when God would restore the fortunes of Israel and all God's people would share in a new embodied creation. The second and third sections of the book explore the understanding of resurrection in the theology of Paul and in early Christianity (both canonical and non-canonical Christian texts). Three points emerge from this study and exegesis of the texts: first, the resurrection occupies a central, rather than marginal, place in early Christian thought; second, Paul and the early Christians believed that the tomb was empty; and third, early Christian reflection about the resurrection marked a significant departure from pagan and Jewish thought. The early Christians believed that Jesus of Nazareth had been raised from the dead. This was no general resurrection. Only one person was involved – and Wright can find no precedent in ancient literature for the view that an individual, let alone a Messiah, might be raised from the dead.

This pattern of argument is common in Wright's work on Christian origins. It is the point where he departs from the consensus of the History of Religions School. He seeks to challenge its emphasis on the continuities between Judaism(s), Hellenism(s) and the emerging early church(es). So he outlines the points of similarity and then identifies the significant points of dissimilarity. Wright uses this principle of dissimilarity to provoke the reader to conclude that something unusual or unexpected had actually happened at the point of Jesus' death. Thus the resurrection of Jesus Christ was without precedent. Something unprecedented must have happened to create the necessary conditions for the Christian modulation of Jewish teaching about the resurrection.

Part IV is probably the most interesting part of the volume. It contains Wright's survey of what the four canonical gospels have to say about the resurrection. Here Wright's mastery of the material, his exegetical skill, his wisdom and scholarship, and his insight into the minds of the evangelists shine through. And yet, it is also the point where some of the inconsistencies of his argument are revealed. For instance, Matthew 27.51–4 records the death of Jesus at the crucifixion, when the veil of the Temple was torn in two (as in Mark). But unlike Mark, Matthew goes on to say that at that precise point there was an earthquake 'and the tombs were opened, and many bodies of the sleeping saints were raised, and going out of the tombs after his arising they went into the holy city and appeared to many'. The problem here is that this passage requires some fairly imaginative exegesis if Wright is to sustain his claim that what made early Christian reflection about the resurrection distinctive was its emphasis on an individual, rather than a general, resurrection. He seems to suggest that Matthew includes this tradition even though it departs from what he really wants to say about the resurrection. Moreover, like a number of New Testament scholars, Wright argues for the historicity of the empty tomb accounts on the grounds that the women play such a central role in bearing witness to the resurrection. Although Paul makes no reference to the women, it would be impossible for Mark to create a tradition, which would hardly serve his apologetic purposes: 'women were simply not acceptable as legal witnesses' (p. 607). Curiously, Wright does not consider or even bother to refute a range of opposing opinions regarding the emergence of this tradition. His own apologetic interests are perhaps most pronounced at this point, but he does not seek to claim that he has 'proved' that the tomb was empty.

He simply asserts that only such a hypothesis will create the sufficient and necessary conditions for the historian to make sense of subsequent historical events.

The historian's task completed, the final section of the book considers the meaning of the resurrection. This is a complex area. One of the threads throughout the book has involved some discussion of human identity, and the different understandings of the relationship between 'soul', 'body' and 'spirit'. Wright speaks of 'transphysicality' to denote the early Christian understanding of the embodied nature of *life after* life after death. And yet given the profound and continuing state of flux which attends our understanding of self and human identity (think of issues like gender, genetics, race, culture, virtual reality, and so on), what kind of discourse about human identity will give expression to the Christian hope of the resurrection in the twenty-first century? At funerals and memorial services, I suspect that the word 'transphysicality' would cause a little consternation and some confusion. There is a pastoral dimension to these questions about the theology of the resurrection that is largely unexplored.

Rather than a detailed and theological exploration of these questions, the final chapters contain a thorough denunciation of the 'brittle scepticism' of Enlightenment historiography (p. 715f.) and also the more wayward and self-indulgent claims of post-modernity. This is good knockabout stuff. Thus Wright asks: 'are we condemned to remain for ever in mutually exclusive closed epistemological circles?' The interesting question is whether the 'critical realism' advocated in Wright's first volume still helps us to chart a middle way. It is perhaps an indication of just how much things have changed in the disciplines of biblical scholarship and critical theory that this question is now more, not less, controversial.

Wright's achievement lies in the way in which he has brought together a vast array of different pieces of the jigsaw that help us to gain a picture of attitudes towards life after death and the resurrection of the dead in the ancient world. He has also confronted biblical scholars with some uncomfortable questions about their willingness, even eagerness, to dismiss the testimony of the early Church. I am persuaded by the overriding argument that the tomb was empty, and yet Wright's work begs some serious questions: What does this mean? Does the simple distinction between Jewish, pagan and Christian world-views do justice to the different contexts and interactions of earliest Christianity? How uniform were early Christian beliefs about the resurrection? Is early Christian discourse about eschatology as consistent and unified as he suggests? How do we make sense of the intermediate state? Is Roman Catholic teaching about 'purgatory' a legitimate development of this tradition? How much room is there for the development of Christian theological discourse about the resurrection?

Some of these questions are addressed in part, but if the book serves to challenge the reader to wrestle again with such questions, Wright will have succeeded in making a major contribution to Anglican reflection about the theology of the resurrection. This is a volume which will sit happily on the bookshelf alongside Peter Carnley's *The Structure of Resurrection Belief,* Oliver O'Donovan's *Resurrection and Moral Order* and Rowan Williams' *Resurrection.*

Will Lamb

Susan Frank Parsons (ed) · *The Cambridge Companion to Feminist Theology* (Cambridge University Press, 2002), 286 pp. Price, £15.95.

There are so many collections mapping the development of feminist theology that one wonders about the wisdom of publishing yet another. However, even on an initial inspection the reader is struck by the depth and breath of scholarship that is contained in this volume. The Cambridge series of 'Companions to Religion' has already provided us with many fine collections, and this current one will certainly enhance the existing list. Though the publishers suggest that the series is intended to provide an introduction to each subject for new readers, many of the essays in this, and indeed other volumes, do require a significant degree of theological literacy. Thus, in the case of the *Cambridge Companion to Feminist Theology*, while each of the essays does cover the emergence of the theological discussion in relation to, for example, the doctrine of the trinity, or to philosophy of religion or to ethics, it also develops these theological themes in important new directions.

The collection is structured in an interesting manner, with Part One gathering essays under the heading of 'The shape of feminist theology' and Part Two introducing 'The themes of feminist theology'. The first part, which looks at the feminist theological inheritance in terms of key methodological approaches, is particularly innovative in terms of its conceptualization. In this section there are essays, for example on 'Feminist theology as intercultural discourse' by Kwok Pui-Lan, 'Feminist theology as theology of religions' by Rita Gross and 'Feminist theology as feminist biblical hermeneutics' by Bridget Gilfillan Upton. The conventional approach would be to identify the feminist contribution to, for example, theology of religions, biblical hermeneutics or philosophy of religion, thereby assessing feminist perspectives in terms of its engagement with existing theological categories. Here, however, the editor takes a different approach, asking each author to focus on frameworks of understanding and methodological issues, in order to disclose the nature of feminist theology itself. As a result there is a freshness about this collection, particularly in these early chapters that foreground methodological matters. It is perhaps unfair to focus on specific essays purely on the basis of their interest to the reviewer. That said, however, of particular interest to this reader were the essays by Kwok Pui-Lan on intercultural discourse and by Pamela Sue Anderson on philosophy of religion. Kwok Pui-Lan's essay accentuates the truly diverse character of feminist theology and explodes the myth that it is a Western, middle-class phenomenon. Moreover, her analysis of the impact of cultural and economic contexts (and particularly of globalization) on the shape of feminist theological discourse is insightful and suggestive. Anderson's meditation on the nature of feminist theology as philosophy is also compelling. Focusing on debates about gender and reason, Anderson covers a tremendous amount of ground in an assured and interesting manner and hints at an emerging epistemology for feminist theology that takes social location seriously.

The second section of the collection focuses on what the editor calls 'themes in feminist theology', with the attention here being given mainly to doctrinal concerns. The excellent essay on 'Feminism and the Trinity' captures the creativity that is characteristic of the best of feminist theology. Here Janet Martin Soskice engages critically with feminist Trinitarian theology, illustrating that the most accomplished feminist reflections are those that are, in the end, utterly traditional. She discusses some of the unhelpful tendencies that some feminist thinking has promoted and is particularly allergic to what she terms the 'sentimentalising of the spirit'. Also in this section is Mercy Amba Oduyoye's essay on Jesus Christ, which takes as the context of feminist theologizing the African theological tradition in all its diversity. Just as in Soskice's essay one gets a sense of the importance of the worshipping church, similarly in this essay the prayer and praxis of the church are represented as playing a vital role in the articulation of African christologies. Other essays in this section are on the Holy Spirit and on creation eschatology as well as church and sacrament, and they provide comprehensive and insightful accounts of the current state of argument. Susan Frank Parsons' own essay, entitled 'Redeeming Ethics', presents a judicious analysis of the dominant themes in feminist ethics. She articulates a highly original approach to feminist ethics in which the theological mode of reflection is accentuated. One looks forward to seeing a fuller development of this approach in the future.

Reading Rosemary Radford Ruether's introductory essay on the emergence of Christian feminist theology through the lens of the essays that follow is an interesting experience. What one is most struck by is how successfully feminist theologians have managed to disrupt the dominant discourse and to insist that theological reflection become more attentive to its gendered character. And this accomplished collection of essays is a testament to the efforts of generations of feminist theologians (women and men) who have insisted that, in addressing the misogyny of the tradition, Christian theology will emerge as a more dynamic and creative discourse.

Linda Hogan

Adrian Hastings · *Oliver Tomkins. The Ecumenical Enterprise*
(London: SPCK, 2001), viii + 184 pp. Price, £50.00. ISBN 0-281-05441-X.

Oliver Tomkins (1908–92), Bishop of Bristol from 1959 to 1975, was one of that generation of post-war leaders of the Church of England who brought to the bench immense experience of the worldwide Church. Unlike, for example, Leslie Brown, who had extensive experience of the mission field in India and then in Uganda, Tomkins' knowledge of worldwide Christianity was formed in an unusual and rather distinctive way – through his involvement at the highest level in the growing ecumenical movement. First as a secretary in SCM, and then, after a Sheffield incumbency during the war, as Assistant Secretary to the World Council of Churches, he built up an amazing network of contacts with European churches in particular. The late Adrian Hastings, in what proved to be his last (and posthumously-published) work, brings Tomkins' ecumenical work into the foreground of this excellent biography.

It is a sad fact of life that ecumenism no longer seems to stir the passions of churchpeople in the way it did in the mid-twentieth century. Hastings' assessment of Tomkins' significance is a finely-balanced one. Tomkins was profoundly committed to the goal of organic unity – that is, the real union into one church of previously separated, confessional or 'denominational' traditions. Despite immense work along these lines, and considerable achievement, still the truth is that certain 'grand' schemes failed (Anglican–Methodist unity being the most obvious example), and that progress came frustratingly slowly. Tomkins felt a strong sense of failure in his later years, as the ecumenical project seemed to run out of steam. And yet, as Hastings points out, what Tomkins held to be the most important ecumenical context – the local church – in point of fact has gradually come to the fore in ecumenical progress over the last three decades.

Tomkins the man emerges from this book as a quietly passionate, confident and engaging man, whose *métier* above all was in ecclesiastical diplomacy, but who brought to all of the organizational tasks he undertook a remarkable ability to respond positively to people of different views and backgrounds. An amateur poet, he was apparently also a proud if sometimes distant family man. Drawing on extensive private papers, Hastings very much conveys the impression of a man of deep if well-hidden feelings, whose life was dominated by what many people would regard as deadening bureaucratic management, and yet who infused that necessary work with humility and dedication. Hastings is at pains to point out that Tomkins was not an original or academic theologian, and in doing so perhaps understates the sense in which the kind of work Tomkins undertook for the WCC, and for Faith and Order, did nevertheless require its own kind of intellectual clarity and brilliance.

For all that, it is probable that Tomkins would not be regarded by many people as amongst the first rank of Anglican leadership in the late twentieth century. Yet that would seem to be unjust and almost certainly stems from the persistent failure of many English Anglicans to realize the momentous change that the ecumenical movement has engendered in currents of Christianity worldwide. Tomkins' personal commitment to local church unity perhaps led him to be over-optimistic, backing the resolution of the Nottingham Conference on Faith and Order in 1964 to press for full and visible unity by 1980. The Conference's commitment to 'areas of ecumenical experiment' made progress but slowly, and yet nevertheless with gathering momentum. Ironically, the pre-eminence of British church leaders in the ecumenical movement (one thinks of Temple, Bell, Oldham and Paton, as well as Tomkins) in the mid-twentieth century may have led to a situation in which the very real progress made at local level in Britain was rarely placed in comparative context. And so impatience grew, without the encouragement that a consideration of the situation in Germany, say, or France, or America might have given. In the emergence of local British ecumenism as a genuinely experimental situation Tomkins played a central role. If – as we should – we then put the question of church unity right back at the very centre of our ecclesial concern, then the part played by certain Anglican church leaders was vital, and Tomkins was up there amongst them.

Jeremy Morris

F. D. Maurice · *The Kingdom of Christ* ([1838], 2 vols. Price
£17.50 each); ***The Prayer Book*** ([1849], 1 vol. Price £17.50);
Theological Essays [1853], 1 vol. Price £19.50). All reprinted
in paperback (Cambridge: James Clarke & Co. [Lutterworth],
2002.

F. D. Maurice (1805–72) was one of the greatest Anglican
theologians of the nineteenth century – some would put
him even higher than Newman (who, after all, repudiated
the Anglican position). He was the champion of the 'compre-
hensiveness' of the Church of England, defender of its liturgy,
founder of Christian Socialism, and an important voice in
articulating a positive response to the rise of biblical criticism
and the challenge of science. Yet his has been a neglected
voice in recent years. His literary style was not the clearest or
most succinct, and his vast output – on one reckoning nearly
five million words – is a forbidding monument. This is a pity,
however, as a number of his books are of exceptional historical
interest, and reward patient study.

James Clarke & Co. have reprinted three of them. *The
Kingdom of Christ* proved in the long run to be by far the most
influential of Maurice's works, admired by Alec Vidler, Michael
Ramsey and Gabriel Hebert, amongst others. It is a plea for
church unity, based on a very broad concept of Catholicity
traced through all the diverse strands of Christian belonging, yet located above all for Maurice in the English 'National
Church'. *The Prayer Book* contains a series of sermons
preached early in 1848, the 'Year of Revolutions'. It is a remarkable argument in favour of the Anglican liturgy as the Church's
best defence against internal division and social conflict. The
Theological Essays secured Maurice's dismissal from his chair
at King's College, London, for his allegedly unorthodox views
on eternal punishment. Yet in fact they are a systematic theology in miniature, addressed to Unitarians as a persuasive in
favour of Trinitarian belief. Maurice's eschatology to a modern
eye looks unexceptionable, if not always clear, yet his social
Trinitarianism will undoubtedly come as a surprise to some
people.

Why read Maurice today? Obviously these will be interesting and useful books for anyone interested in the history of Anglican theology. James Clarke & Co. have put within the range of the ordinary book-buyer three Anglican 'classics' unobtainable for years. Despite the faults of Maurice's style, and the many contradictions and confusions in his published work, there is an immense breadth to his theology that remains startling today. He interweaves prayer, scriptural reasoning, historical analysis, and pastoral sensitivity in a creative way, prompting furious disagreement and passionate assent by turns. Reading him requires persistence – but it certainly rewards that.

Jeremy Morris

Steven Croft · *Transforming Communities. Re-imagining the Church for the 21st Century* (London: DLT, 2002), xiii + 226 pp. Price, £10.95 pbk.

After twenty years of varied Christian ministry Steven Croft gives us the fruit of his reflections, experience and research. Indeed, such is his generosity that in Chapter 1 he lays before us the answer to Church decline (as he sees it) through the development of small groups within the current structures of the Church.

Having given us the answer, he then elaborates on the causes of our present malaise. The analysis is wide-ranging and thorough. It invites our confidence, for he can be objective and critical of his own spiritual tradition, if necessary, and of certain evangelical failures to kickstart church growth. He warns us of the use of 'vision' in the secular market place: now handed back to the church, it has been distorted so that there is a danger of the church looking for growth and profit. Rather, in Croft's opinion, growth must be natural and organic if new structures are to take root and develop.

Croft's exegesis is conducted sensitively, but I found myself more relaxed with his historical survey of Christian groups, beginning with the patterns emerging in the *Acts of the Apostles*, the earliest house churches, through the monastic movement, the Methodist class system, to Latin American soul groups and the house groups beloved of so many parishes today. The use of groups for basic Christian activity has a strong pedigree and Croft encourages us to see them as units of transformation.

There is much here that makes good sense. We are all aware – and have been for some time – of the evidence of decline staring us in the face. Here is a courageous vision that takes us beyond the hand-wringing stage into a future where the ecclesiastical landscape is not changed unrecognizably but allows the Church to grow with the aid of small transforming communities. So down to earth is this vision that the final part of the book leads through a step-by-step approach to the answer. The vision extolled in this book will find a resonance around the country among many of the schemes currently being developed, as churches and dioceses plan for the future.

In the week that this book was published I shared a conference platform with Steven Croft, but we were at opposite ends of the programme. I'm sorry I didn't stay to hear his gloss on this vision. I am sure we will have more from his pen in this vein, for I do believe he is on to something crucial and quite consonant with the Gospel. We may not always like what he sets before us – and some of his diagrams in the book are challenging! – but there is a sense and a depth to this work which defies glib objections.

Christopher Armstrong

The Reviewers

Christopher Armstrong is Dean of Blackburn · **Linda Hogan** works at the Irish School of Ecumenics, Dublin · **Will Lamb** is Anglican Chaplain to the University of Sheffield · **Jeremy Morris** is Dean of Trinity Hall, Cambridge, and Editor of *Third Millennium*.